"*She Leads* is the perfect primer for parents committed to raising the next generation of female leaders our world so desperately needs. It's a blueprint for empowering young women to redefine success and remake the world in their image."
— Arianna Huffington,
Founder & CEO, Thrive Global

She LEADS

A Practical Guide
for Raising Girls
Who Advocate,
Influence, and Lead

Tim Jordan, M.D.

She Leads
A Practical Guide for Raising Girls Who Advocate, Influence, and Lead
Tim Jordan, M.D.
Children & Families, Inc.

Published by Children & Families, Inc., St. Louis, MO
Copyright ©2020 Tim Jordan, M.D.
All rights reserved.

No part of this publication may be reproduced, stored in a retrieval system, or transmitted in any form or by any means, electronic, mechanical, photocopying, recording, scanning, or otherwise, except as permitted under Section 107 or 108 of the 1976 United States Copyright Act, without the prior written permission of the Publisher. Requests to the Publisher for permission should be addressed to Permissions Department, Children & Families, Inc. and Anne@drtimjordan.com.

Limit of Liability/Disclaimer of Warranty: While the publisher and author have used their best efforts in preparing this book, they make no representations or warranties with respect to the accuracy or completeness of the contents of this book and specifically disclaim any implied warranties of merchantability or fitness for a particular purpose. No warranty may be created or extended by sales representatives or written sales materials. The advice and strategies contained herein may not be suitable for your situation. You should consult with a professional where appropriate. Neither the publisher nor author shall be liable for any loss of profit or any other commercial damages, including but not limited to special, incidental, consequential, or other damages.

Names, characters, businesses, places, events and incidents are either the products of the author's imagination or used in a fictitious manner. Any resemblance to actual persons, living or dead, or actual events is purely coincidental.

Editor: Karyn Williams
Cover and Interior design: Davis Creative, DavisCreative.com

Library of Congress Cataloging-in-Publication Data
Library of Congress Control Number: 2019916952
Tim Jordan
She Leads: A Practical Guide for Raising Girls Who Advocate, Influence, and Lead

ISBN: 978-0-9771051-4-4

Library of Congress subject headings:

1. FAM034000 Family & Relationships /Parenting/ General   2. EDU032000 EDUCATION / Leadership   3. SEL027000 Self-Help Personal Growth / Success

ATTENTION CORPORATIONS, UNIVERSITIES, COLLEGES AND PROFESSIONAL ORGANIZATIONS: Quantity discounts are available on bulk purchases of this book for educational, gift purposes, or as premiums for increasing magazine subscriptions or renewals. Special books or book excerpts can also be created to fit specific needs. For information, please contact Children & Families, Inc. 300 Chesterfield Center, Suite 255, Chesterfield, MO 63017; ph 636-530-1883 or email Anne@drtimjordan.com.

Gratitude Page

First and foremost, I'm forever grateful for the honor of hearing the stories of girls and young women in my counseling practice, retreats, and summer camps. They have taught me so much about what's going on in the lives on girls today. And it has been an honor to be a part of their growing up, especially watching as they blossomed into incredible leaders. Their courage, vulnerability, and energy give me the fuel to continue my work each and every day. Many of the ideas in this book came from my experiences working with them for the past 30 years.

I'm grateful for my wife Anne's unconditional love and support, especially when I start a new project or book because she knows it will bring her more work as well. She has been with me with every new venture, taking care of our business and all of the detail work, allowing me to focus on things like this book.

I also appreciate the people who reviewed the book along the way, offering ideas and direction. I am especially grateful for the feedback received from my son John and his wife Isa, my son TJ, and Anna Bushlack. Many thanx also to my editor Karyn Williams who always makes my words more readable.

Finally, I'm grateful to be alive. While finishing up this book, I underwent open heart surgery to repair some cardiac congenital anomalies and their effects. The love and support I received from family, friends, campers, camp staff, and others was overwhelming, in a great way. I have never felt so loved and supported, and their love certainly aided my recovery. I wouldn't have finished this book without their support.

Also by Tim Jordan, M.D.

Letters from My Grandfather: Timeless Wisdom for a Life Worth Living; 2018

Sleeping Beauties, Awakened Women: Guiding the Transformation of Adolescent Girls; 2015

Keeping Your Family Grounded When You Are Flying By the Seat of Your Pants, 2005

Food Fights and Bedtime Battles: A Working Parent's Guide to Negotiating Daily Power Struggles; 2001

What I Learned at Summer Camp: About Understanding and Loving Our Children; 1994

Table of Contents

Gratitude Page... iii
Introduction: Girls Who Want More......................... 1
Chapter 1: Redefining Power and Leadership 5
Chapter 2: Why Girls Become Constrained 7
Chapter 3: How Girls Give Their Power Away 13
Chapter 4: Inner Directed 17
Chapter 5: Motivation... 19
Chapter 6: Moral Compass 25
Chapter 7: Intuition 29
Chapter 8: Value Passion Where You Find It................ 35
Chapter 9: Social-Emotional Intelligence 39
Chapter 10: Self-Awareness 41
Chapter 11: Conflict Resolution and a Win-Win Mentality.. 47
Chapter 12: Overcoming Fears 51
Chapter 13: Generosity.. 53
Chapter 14: Overcoming Adversity........................... 55
Chapter 15: Connections...................................... 61
Chapter 16: Sacred Spaces 67
Chapter 17: Brave Leaders.................................... 69
Chapter 18: Powerful Girls Misunderstood 71
Chapter 19: Different Kinds of Leaders...................... 75
Chapter 20: Paradigm Shift About Courage 79

Chapter 21: Step into a Leader's Shoes 81
Chapter 22: Assertive vs. Aggressive 83
Chapter 23: Keeping Your Power 87
Chapter 24: Un-Words 93
Chapter 25: Opportunities for Advocacy 95
Chapter 26: Where Do We Go from Here 99
Notes: Leadership book 103
Also by Dr. Tim Jordan M.D. 107
About the Author 109

Introduction: Girls Who Want More

If your actions inspire others to dream more, learn more, do more, and become more, you are a leader.
　　　　　　　　　　　　　　　　–John Quincy Adams

What do Eleanor Roosevelt, Bobbi Brown, Malala Yousafzai, Jane Goodall, Ruth Bader Ginsburg, Margaret Mead and Belle from *Beauty and the Beast* have in common? They were all women who wanted more—and so do many of your daughters. A 2019 study by Plan International[2] surveyed more than 10,000 girls and young women in more than 70 countries about leadership. They found that 76% of girls globally aspire to be a leader in their country, community and career. So, how do you parent girls to fully bloom into strong, fearless women who create more?

In *Beauty and the Beast*, Belle lives in a quiet town, where she sees the same people and has the same routine every day. The townspeople describe her as "odd, dazed, peculiar, and never part of any crowd, with her head up on some cloud." Belle ignores them all and sings out, "I want much more than this provincial life."

What do many powerful girls have in common with Belle? She says it well: "I want someone to understand, I want more than they have planned!" Girls want to break free from limiting stereotypes and become their best selves. The girls interviewed in the Plan International study felt that gender discrimination, blatant sexism and stereotyping were all barriers to their growth. Girls want to have a voice, be heard, push out of their comfort zones, pursue their passions, and for many, become a leader. As Ariel sings out in The Little Mermaid, "I want more."

We hear a lot about the benefits of empowering girls, and we want our daughters to be effective, influential leaders. Yet we receive very little instruction on how to actually parent girls to that end. And what does an "empowered girl" actually look and act like? What does an influential girl look like at age 5, 12, 15, 18, 21? There is also a global need for a different kind of leadership, yet there is scant discussion about the qualities necessary to make this change. Today, girls around the world have a different definition of leadership[2] that emphasizes collaboration to bring about positive change.

In school, the girls typically labeled as leaders are the student council president, team captains, the queen bee, and the pretty, popular girls. And the people our country holds up as heroes are often males who are soldiers, athletes, or first responders. Yet the vast majority of girls don't fit these roles, in either school or the 'real world,' and so their style of being powerful is overlooked. They aren't acknowledged for who they are and what they bring to their peers and community.

This book describes three leadership qualities that are most in need today: being inner-directed, having high social-emotional intelligence and being assertive. We are not giving girls the awareness and skills to develop these traits at home or school. I will delve into topics like self-motivation, learning win-win conflict resolution skills, accessing and trusting your intuition, and pushing through anxiety and fears. You will take away very practical parenting strategies and tools to help develop these traits and more like them in your daughter.

The majority of the girls I work with through my counseling practice, school programs, weekend retreats and summer camps

Introduction: Girls Who Want More

are middle or upper class and Caucasian. But it is also my experience that girls of color and those who come from disadvantaged backgrounds resonate with these ideas as well. I suspect the leaders of the future will be a much more diverse lot than we currently have; the tide already has started turning in that direction.

This book will be your guide in raising strong, confident, passionate, influential women who become successful and powerful initiators of change.

Chapter 1

Redefining Power and Leadership

A lone vehicle slowly approaches a checkpoint at the Israeli-Palestine border. When the guards at the gate walk toward the car, the driver jumps out, shouting expletives at them. He is angry at the inconvenience of stopping and their suspicions of him. This is one of the moments that can potentially explode into violence if not handled properly.

Maj. Gen. Orna Barbivai of the Israeli army understands the value of feminine leadership traits. Israeli women are conscripted into the military just like men. When the amount of conflicts at the Palestinian border had risen, Barbivai was put in charge. She decided to station female soldiers at the front lines because she had discovered that women often approached tense situations with more empathy and patience. These qualities are invaluable in dangerous areas along the border where traffic flows in and out of Palestine. Because of the way female soldiers excelled at negotiating to avoid conflict, like in the aforementioned situation, the disputes at the checkpoints decreased significantly.

I read about Barbivai in John Gerzema and Michael D'Antonio's book, *The Athena Doctrine*[1]. The authors surveyed 64,000 citizens in 13 nations to discover how they defined traditional masculine and feminine leadership traits, and each nationality was consistent in its perceptions. People around the world reported their aversions to traditional masculine thinking and behaviors, including codes of control, competition, aggression and black-and-white thinking. Across age, gender and culture, people believed feminine traits correlate more strongly with making the world a better place. For more details on their findings, read the book.

People want patient leaders who can connect on a personal level, who handle conflicts with reason versus ideology, and who can think win-win and listen to all sides of an issue. They also want leaders who are intuitive and proficient at collaboration and cooperation, who demonstrate flexibility, humility and candor, and who value connectedness and vulnerability. The girls and women from 70 countries in the Plan International Study[2] revealed their most important leadership qualities are striving for social and gender justice, making decisions collectively, and leading in a way that empowers and helps others.

Our challenge is to find ways to encourage and acknowledge these traits in children. We also need to raise awareness of how we may unconsciously inhibit these virtues.

Chapter 2

Why Girls Become Constrained

The egg of an eagle somehow found its way to a corner of a barn where a hen was hatching her own eggs. Soon the baby eaglet hatched along with the other chickens. As time passed, the eaglet experienced a desire to fly. She would ask her mother, the hen, "When can I learn to fly?" Well, the poor hen had neither the ability to fly nor the slightest notion of how to teach a bird to do so. But she was ashamed to admit this, so she would say, "Not yet, my child, not yet. I shall teach you when you are ready." Months passed, and the young eagle began to suspect that its mother did not know how to fly, but she could not get herself to break loose and fly on her own. Her own aspirations had become confused with the gratitude she felt toward the bird that hatched her.

Parents, teachers and society send messages, sometimes unintentionally, that condition girls to want less and to hide their light. The following are examples of how girls can become constrained.

Good girl conditioning: Girls are still absorbing old messages that tell them to be 'good girls.' When I've asked girls on my retreats to make a list of all of the qualities of a good girl, they come up with traits such as:
- polite, passive, sweet and perfect
- obedient and follows the rules
- doesn't stand out, not too loud, doesn't make waves
- selfless pleaser who puts other's needs first
- waits her turn and lets others make decisions

- always happy and doesn't get angry
- does not argue or disagree
- always tries her best
- pretty

That's a disturbing list for sure. For more information on this phenomenon, read Rachel Simmons' book, *The Curse of the Good Girl*[3].

Molly is a girl I saw in my counseling practice who received a good girl message at age 8. She was with her mom at a parent teacher conference in third grade when she overheard her teacher say that Molly was too bossy and if she didn't change, she'd never make any friends. The words stung a lot, and her response was to shut down. I saw Molly in counseling at age 17 because she couldn't make decisions. After allowing other people to make choices for her for years, she had lost touch with her needs and desires. Molly also carried around the fear of being judged if she spoke out or expressed what she wanted.

Mixed messages: Along with the good girl conditioning comes a host of mixed messages that result in girls feeling confused. Girls have described experiencing these from parents, teachers and other adults in their lives. For example, when a young girl goes to a family gathering, most of the comments directed to her are about her looks: "Look how pretty you are." "You look so cute in your outfit." Little boys tend to be acknowledged for how big they've gotten, or how strong they are.

Another example of an adult's influence concerns the concept of a fixed versus a growth mindset. According to Carol Dweck's research[4], a fixed mindset is when people believe abilities are fixed, that you are born with gifts that can't be changed. Girls more so than boys tend to have a fixed mindset, especially with math.

When girls with this mentality encounter a challenging task, they are more likely to believe the stereotype that boys are better at math and give up. However, girls with a growth mindset believe that strength in a certain subject comes from an acquired set of skills that can be improved with practice. In the face of challenges, they are far more likely to persist and not succumb to limiting stereotypes. Dweck's recommendation to parents and educators is to "rethink what implicit and explicit messages are being sent to young girls about achievement." She also believes that a lack of female role models in STEM careers has made it harder for young girls to see themselves in those careers. Girls hear that they can be whatever they want, but they actually receive a more limited view of their potential. For more on this concept, read Dweck's book.

Here are some conflicting thoughts girls deal with:
- Be smart, but not too smart or opinionated.
- Be confident, but don't be too assertive because you might cause conflict or jealousy.
- Be a leader but stay mostly behind the scenes.
- Be nice, but also be competitive and ambitious.
- Be successful but not 'all that.'
- Be powerful even though you'll risk being judged as a bitch.
- Be liked, accepted and popular, but be yourself and authentic.
- Don't make your friends mad, but stand up for yourself.
- Take care of yourself, but put others' needs first.
- You can do whatever you want, but you can't be yourself.

Girls learn pretty quickly to stay in line or there will be negative repercussions. It reminds me of the Japanese proverb: The nail that stands up gets hammered down.

Fear of judgments: The following are fears girls have expressed to me that cause them to not speak out:

- don't want to displease or disappoint others
- might be rejected or ostracized
- won't fit in or will lose popularity if they say something wrong
- may end up alone, lonely and isolated
- no boy or man will want them
- could be wrong, fail or look stupid
- might be persecuted and judged for thinking/ being different

These are just a few reasons why girls might choose to hold back, not speak their truth, give in to others and not fully blossom. It is critical to be aware of this unconscious good girl conditioning so you don't perpetuate it. One constructive way to do this is to make a list of good girl qualities with your daughter and talk about how unrealistic many of them are. Discuss which ones she might want to adopt and which ones she will disregard.

Empathize with the challenge of sorting through the mixed messages she faces. Just becoming aware of them takes away a lot of their power. Help her reframe the messages and consciously choose where she stands with each of them. For example, your daughter might be afraid to confront a friend who has been talking behind her back. Here is how the conversation might go:

Mom: "It sounds like you are upset with Lauren because you heard she was spreading rumors about you. Have you talked to her about it?"

Daughter: "No, not yet."

Mom: "What's your fear about confronting her?"

Daughter: "You know how popular she is. I'm worried she may get mad at me and not want to be my friend."

Mom: "It makes sense why you might worry about that. Can I give you another way of looking at it?"

Daughter: "Sure."

Mom: "A good friend would listen to your concerns and respect your wishes. If Lauren blows up and avoids you, she's telling you what kind of friend she is, a lower level friend who you can't trust. I understand how hard it is to move on, even from bad friends, but you might want to think about what kind of friends you want and deserve."

When girls share their fears, it takes away much of their energy and power.

Let me share another example of an older girl I counseled. Chloe felt conflicted about choosing a college. She always had been extremely conscious of not wanting to disappoint people, especially her parents. Having attended a very small high school, Chloe had the urge to go to a mid-size college with more diversity. Her parents were steering her toward a small, liberal arts college of 1,400 students. When I asked Chloe where she had decided to go, she said, with little conviction or emotion, that she had "settled on the small school." I encouraged her to visit the two schools that most appealed to *her*, choose one, understand why *she* selected that university, and then speak to her family in a firm but respectful manner. It was clearly time for Chloe to stand up for herself even if her parents disagreed. Otherwise, it would inevitably cost her a lifetime of regret for not following her path.

Raising awareness and giving girls healthier views on these issues will go a long way toward overcoming them. In the next chapter, I will explain the many ways girls mistakenly give up their power.

Chapter 3

How Girls Give Their Power Away

There are many ways both girls and women give their power away to others. The following are the most common.

They act like they don't care when they do. The automatic response for many girls when questioned about what they want is to say I don't care or redirect the question to someone else. I tell girls that this response teaches people that what they have to say is not important, and therefore *they* are not important. This becomes a bad habit that can lead to feelings of resentment and unhappiness.

They don't ask for what they want. Isa is a sensitive 7-year-old who was annoyed with a boy who kept pestering her. She told him to stop on many occasions and finally went to her teacher for help. Her teacher's response was to tell Isa to just mind her own business, causing her to feel dismissed and unimportant. From that day forward, she never raised her hand in class or asked people for what she needed to avoid feeling that way again.

They make decisions so people will like them or not get upset. The female brain[5] has been wired to avoid conflict, resulting in girls not wanting to anger or disappoint people. Too often this results in them not getting what they want or having their needs met.

They spend a lot of time and energy trying to make everyone happy. Abby, 14, grew up with a younger brother with Down syndrome. He almost died three times, causing the family to focus on his needs. Because of this, Abby came to believe that other people's needs were more important than hers, and eventually, that she shouldn't have needs. She has become great at taking care of everyone else but herself.

They worry about judgment from others. Lauren gave up orchestra in seventh grade because her new popular friend group told her that cheer was much cooler. Many girls worry so much about what other people think that they become controlled by judgments, real or imagined. It can affect how they dress, talk, who they hang out with, and what activities they choose.

They compare themselves with others: Sanaa, 13, hates how she looks, especially when she compares herself to her friends. She told me her nose was too big, her face was too wide, she hates and obsesses over her fingernails, and she feels ugly and weird. Her quote says it all: "I feel like a single Fruit Loop in a bowl of Cheerios." I've had girls at my summer camps make up a list of ways that they compare themselves to their peers. The lists are incredibly long, including statements that their friends are smarter, prettier, hotter, more athletic, more popular, taller, thinner, funnier, stronger, more outgoing, braver, and more attractive and talented to name a few. I tell them comparisons are a bad trap because in their minds, they will always find someone who is 'something-er' than them.

They give up their true selves. Christina lost her friend group in both fifth and eighth grade. She began high school wearing a lot of makeup, acting cool and hanging out with the 'wild' kids. I saw her because she was feeling depressed, a symptom of not being herself. It's hard for girls to resist the pressure of giving up themselves to fit in and be accepted during times they feel insecure.

They avoid conflicts.: Girls resist confronting friends and handling conflicts directly because they fear losing their friends and ending up alone. They act like the conflict is no big deal or they avoid the other person, allowing bad feelings to fester and creating more drama. This oftentimes includes apologizing when they have done nothing wrong in order to try to salvage the friendship. They don't stand up for themselves, set boundaries or speak their truth. Girls tend to err on the side of being liked versus making waves, and they often don't work through conflicts.

They allow words to hurt them. Any time girls allow words, teasing or rumors to affect their feelings, they are giving their power away. They are letting other people be in charge of their mood, emotions and reactions.

They don't trust their intuition. Being too focused on pleasing others, not disappointing people, trying to fit in, and wanting to be liked leads girls to make decisions for reasons other than what is right for them. They learn to ignore, not trust, and not act on their intuition.

Girls who want the courage to lead and take initiative need to be aware of the ways they may be giving away their power. In a later chapter, I will explain how to teach your daughters to keep their power.

Chapter 4

Inner Directed

I can honestly say that I was never affected by the question of success being an undertaking. If I felt it was the right thing to do, I was for it, regardless of the possible outcome.
–Golda Meir

The following are examples of what it looks like for a leader to be inner-directed.
- They are self-motivated and don't need people pushing them or motivating them to accomplish their goals.
- Their decisions are based on their own moral compass.
- They set their own bar and are willing to take unpopular paths.
- They know how to quiet themselves, go inward, connect with and trust their intuition and urges, and use those to guide decisions.
- They don't allow themselves to be hurt by criticism or outside opinions.
- They are free to be themselves because they don't care what other people think about them.

If that sounds like a tall order, you're right. The next four chapters offer suggestions for how to parent your children so they develop these traits.

Chapter 5

Motivation

After two years at two different universities, a young woman, Bobbi, decided college wasn't for her. Instead of forcing her to go back to school, her mom asked what she was passionate about. She answered, "Makeup." She transferred to Emerson College in Boston, even though they had no cosmetology major. Bobbi thought she wanted to do theater makeup, so the school let her design her own concentration working with the theater, TV, photography and film departments. Bobbi took charge of her fate, and she continued to live with that philosophy from then on.

"I left college with a B.A. in fine arts in makeup and a minor in photography, but what I really left with was the knowledge that it was all up to me," she says. "Everything in life, everything, is what you put into it. There are so many options for how you live your life and make a career for yourself."

The young woman, Bobbi Brown[6], eventually became the founder and chief creative officer of her own company, Bobbi Brown Cosmetics. It was her unwillingness to sell out and do the 'normal' college path that ensured her eventual success.

The following are tools to support your child's self-motivation.

Switch from a paradigm of "How do I motivate my child?" to "How can I support her intrinsic motivation?" Everything your kids do has intrinsic, built-in motivation. There are inherent positive feelings from doing things like playing soccer, building with Legos, playing guitar, solving a friendship conflict or being accepted into college. Your job is to get out of the way of them feeling these emotions. You distract kids from the intrinsic benefits any time you reward them for doing things; they become so focused on the prize that they don't internalize the sense of a job well done.

Contingent rewards, like saying, "If you do __ then you'll get __," take away internal motivation because it requires them to forfeit some of their autonomy. They end up doing it for *your* reasons. Students who are rewarded have their creativity minimized, tend to do only what is needed to get the reward and no more, and avoid taking risks and challenging themselves. They subsequently become less generous than those simply acknowledged for being a kind person. For more on this, read the research compiled by Alfie Kohn[7], as well as Daniel Pink in his book, *Drive*[8].

Ask how they feel about their work. When your 4-year-old asks if you like the picture she drew, resist praising her creation. ("That's so beautiful, let's put it on the refrigerator.") Instead, ask her, "What do *you* think of your picture?" Your question causes her to go inward and ask herself what she likes about her drawing, and her response may surprise you. She might describe why she colored the hair purple or how she liked using every color in the box. Your job then becomes mirroring back what she shares. "Sounds like you love to be creative and use fun colors for people's hair! I love how focused you get when you are coloring. I can tell it's something you love to do." This allows kids to internalize their good feelings about their artwork, and that intrinsic motivation always will be there for them to access.

A high school art teacher told me when he started asking seniors what they liked about their creations, their responses shocked him. Most walked away acting embarrassed and saying they'd do it over if he didn't like it. He realized in those moments that the students had been in school for 12 years and no one had ever asked them what they thought of their work. Don't wait until your kids are seniors; start today.

Give kids greater autonomy. Anyone who has a choice about what they are doing will be more motivated to do it. Being able to choose their activities results in kids being more focused, inspired and enthusiastic. This higher level of engagement is essential for kids to develop the grit and persistence to keep at the task until completion. The 10,000-hour rule states that to attain mastery of your craft, you need to put in at least 10,000 hours of what is referred to as deep practice. Independence will allow kids to become totally consumed with whatever they are doing. When they are passionate about their activity, the activity itself and their efforts become the reward.

In Dan Coyle's book, *The Talent Code*[9], he describes the concept of 'deep practice.' His research found that successful people practice differently. They experience moments of slow, fitful struggle, and when they make a mistake, they stop, look and think carefully before taking the next step. Their progress becomes a matter of small failures. Successful people practice purposefully at the edge of their abilities so that they will mess up. Struggling in targeted areas makes them smarter because it forces them to slow down, make errors and correct them. That is deep practice.

In addition, any time we practice anything, our brain produces a substance called myelin that wraps around nerve fibers. The more myelin your neural circuits have, the better it insulates nerve fibers and the faster signals run through the brain. This makes our movements and thoughts quicker and more accurate; thus, we become better at that task. You need autonomy, persistence, grit and passion to become really good at something because you must keep practicing to fire the brain circuits to continuously produce more myelin. Anders Ericsson's original research thus stated that leaders in every field require around 10,000 hours of committed, deliberate, deep practice. I would add that they also require autonomy.

Ask kids why they like an activity. In the documentary *Jane*[10], Jane Goodall shared that she started dreaming of living in Africa as a young girl. She always loved animals and being outdoors, and she dreamed of being a man because she believed men could do things like go to Africa and work with animals. In her early years of research, Jane didn't give up even though it took months for the chimps to allow her close enough for observations. "Once there, I knew I belonged to the forest," she says. "This is where I was meant to be." Jane was describing her passion, her calling.

In a *60 Minutes* interview, actress Jennifer Lawrence described how she loved performing and inventing stories as a young girl. She felt lost at school. She struggled and never felt smart. Jennifer dreamed of becoming an actress and was discovered by a talent scout on a trip to New York. When she read her first script, she felt like she was in the right place. "I read the script, and I knew exactly what it would look like if someone felt that way," she says. "It was something I felt confident about. I got this overwhelming feeling of, 'I get this, this is what I was meant to do.'"

Ask your daughter why she loves to draw, go to school, play soccer, volunteer, work, or participate in theater or dance. Her response will be a window into her intrinsic motivation. Nine-year-old Abby told me she enjoys dancing because she loves the costumes and being on stage, where she can be free. Azoriah, 17, loves musical theater because she is happy telling a story through song and dance. She appreciates taking the audience on a journey.

If your daughter says she loves soccer because of the competition, performing in front of crowds and the teamwork, this passion can be transferred to other arenas as well where she may succeed. Again, mirror back what your daughter shares so she can internalize why she is passionate about something. You will learn a lot about your kids and what makes them tick this way

Chapter 6

Moral Compass

The highest reward for a person's toil is not what they get for it, but what they become by it.
—John Ruskin

The female brain[11] is wired to connect and to avoid conflict. For 150,000 years, women and their offspring who were in a group had a much better chance of survival. A female who got into conflicts might get kicked out of the tribe, and that meant death. Girls tell me losing a friend feels like a death to them, and they will do whatever it takes to maintain friendships.

Unfortunately, that can translate into behaviors such as: becoming a pleaser, not wanting to disappoint people, and making decisions based on wanting to be liked or not making people mad. We need leaders who can transcend this external orientation and make decisions based on their moral compass.

Ray, 13, was depressed and confused. Her friend group had become pretty wild, drinking alcohol and sneaking boys into parties. She went along with it because they were popular and her only friends, but their behaviors troubled her. At one of my retreats, she came to accept what it would cost to stay with these girls, and she found the courage to take a stand. She left the group and went through a short period of being isolated and lonely. Within a few weeks, though, she found new friends who shared her same values, and she was on her way.

Like Ray, your daughters need to become conscious of how they may be predisposed to avoid conflict and not be true to themselves. Read the book *The Female Brain*[11] together to better understand how their brains work. Help girls become aware of what it will cost them to not be authentic. If you ask them how it feels when they make choices based on external influences, you will hear answers like sad, confused, angry, resentful, empty, numb, and out of integrity. For many girls, that awareness alone provides the motivation to change.

I regularly have girls make a list of qualities they deem important of a best friend. Their lists often include traits like being kind, accepting, trustworthy, a good listener, and inclusive. Like Ray, when they compare the list with their friend group, they often notice how many of their 'friends' don't measure up to the qualities that are most important to them. It's an eye opener that makes it easier to move onto healthier friends and not worry about what everyone else thinks. I encourage girls to start looking for new friends who match their list. This is a good example of making a decision based on what's right for you.

Indirect lessons can be invaluable. Use characters from books, TV shows and movies or people you know to demonstrate points you want to make. If you see someone succumbing to peer pressure and making decisions based on externals, ask your daughter how she thinks that girl might feel. Have her get in that person's shoes and view the situation from her perspective. Ask her if she's ever been in that position before and, if so, how she handled it. It's oftentimes easier to hear parents' wisdom through an example that's not your own.

Notice times when your daughter has the courage to speak up even when it's hard, and acknowledge her for it. You could say, "I love how you can remain true to yourself even when it's unpopular." Or, "That took a lot of courage to stand up for what you knew was right; how did you do that?" Describing the process of being powerful will help her internalize the lesson and experience it even more deeply.

Teach your daughter that when she takes a stand or speaks her truth that some people will think she's the greatest thing since sliced bread. Others will judge and criticize her because of their own issues. She'll have to be ready for all kinds of reactions. Remind her that she is never responsible for other people's feelings or reactions. Show her examples of people who bravely did the right thing despite pressures to follow the crowd. For examples, I love the characters Atticus Finch from *To Kill a Mockingbird*, Katniss Everdeen from *The Hunger Games*, and Moana.

Taylor Swift[12] was offered a development deal with RCA Records at the age of 14, but they wanted her to record covers. Taylor insisted on writing and recording her own songs, and bravely opted not to sign. Even at that young age, she declined advice from adults experienced in songwriting. Her producer Ryan Tedder said, "Artists who are the most successful are the ones who will tell me to my face, 'No, you're wrong' about a song." That determination to follow her truth has been extremely successful for Taylor Swift.

Strong leaders should have the ability to shut out the conflicting noise and opinions around them. They should be able to make decisions that are criticized and unpopular. Those in charge need to develop thick skin that allows them to not care about what others think. Oftentimes what's most important is not to be liked but to do the right thing. Girls especially need guidance in these areas as they are wired to connect and avoid conflict. They need more awareness about how detrimental it is to take criticism personally, and to not speak their truth for fear of ruffling feathers.

I will talk in the next chapter about teaching your daughter to go inward, access her intuition, and know what's right for her.

Chapter 7

Intuition

Dorothy Wharburton[13] won an essay contest at age 14, and the prize was a book about women scientists. The stories inspired her to think that someday she could accomplish that success as well. Dorothy taught herself to type because she thought she could become a secretary to a great scientist. After earning a Ph.D., she got a job as a research associate in the OB-GYN department at Columbia University where her husband worked. No one was interested in the problem of miscarriages, but Dorothy got the urge to research the issue despite no initial support. Eventually, she got backing from the director of the hospital, and Dorothy developed one of the first genetic diagnostic laboratories in the country. She became a leader in her field by trusting her intuition.

The concept of intuition is an important aspect of leadership for several reasons. It includes the ability to trust your gut when making tough decisions. This awareness requires the capacity to quiet yourself and go inward to know what's right. Intuition also means having an awareness of your urges and following through on them. One way to teach kids to be in touch with and trust their intuition is through self-quieting. Young people today need to learn how to slow down despite living in a noisy, distracting world. Techniques to achieve this calm state of mind include:

- Breath work: Sit quietly and focus on breathing through your nose. Count to five as you inhale, hold the breath 1 second, then very slowly exhale as you count down from five. You also can breathe in for 5 seconds, hold the breath for 5-8 seconds, and then slowly exhale. If your mind wanders, refocus on breathing and counting. Just a few minutes of this brings a sense of calm and relaxation.

- Nature: Kids who play outside[14] are smarter, happier, more attentive and less anxious than kids who spend more time indoors. Spending time in green space[15, 16] calms us down and reduces mental fatigue. Being outdoors is a great way to get grounded.
- Journaling: Regularly writing down your thoughts and feelings has many benefits. For one, the act of venting on the page can lighten your load and leave you feeling calmer. Secondly, girls tell me it's hard to process problems because they have so many thoughts swirling in their heads. Writing your thoughts down allows you to look at each issue individually so you don't feel overwhelmed. Journaling becomes a rewarding way to quiet your brain and figure out what you want and need. Encourage your daughter to give it a try for one week and see if it helps. Remind her that like any skill, you get better at it the more you practice.
- Arts and crafts: Any form of art can help self-quiet. One suggestion is adult coloring books, which can be both therapeutic and fun. Encourage your daughter to draw, paint or sculpt as a way to destress. I've had many girls take up knitting or crocheting for the same purpose.
- Music: Listening to relaxing music or playing an instrument can be calming. I read a story about how Albert Einstein used to play violin in the middle of the night whenever he got stuck working on his theorems. Playing helped clear his mind and stimulate his creativity.

- Apps: Guide your kids to use any of the new self-calming apps on the market. A few examples are: Headspace, Calm, Nature Melody, Mindfulness for Children, HelloMind, Free Relaxing Nature Sounds and Spa Music, and Breathe2Relax.
- Un-Words: We all need to carve out time when we are undisturbed and unplugged from technology. Have the whole family commit to periods when everyone is disconnected from all devices. You will be less distracted and more present with each other. In addition, you will allow your brain to rest and destress, all of which will calm you down.
- Model these: Kids will follow your example, so whatever quieting strategies you want them to adopt, practice yourself or as a family.

The second way to trust your intuition is through reflection. Once you've become quiet, it's easier to access your inner world. Soul-searching, reflection, contemplation and daydreaming are lost arts in this busy, externally driven world. Teach your kids to ask themselves questions like: What am I feeling today? What do I need? What feels right to me? What does my heart say is the best decision? Encourage them to write these thoughts into a journal and regularly go back and read what they wrote and add to it. It's a helpful way to make decisions or work through challenges. Albert Einstein's quote fits well here: *"When you follow intuition, the solutions come to you, and you don't know how or why."*

Any time we come to a fork in the road and need to make a choice between right and wrong, an internal alarm goes off as a warning to check in with ourselves. Have your daughter go back to the last time she made a bad decision and recall when her alarm went off. How did she experience it? Common answers are a pit in the stomach, tightening in the chest, heart pounding, sweating, racing thoughts, and feeling anxious or nauseous. Since she chose to ignore the signs in that moment, have her figure out why. Finally, help her take action so the next time that decision arises, she will make a better choice. Teach girls to always respect this alarm; it's there to keep them safe. If they have practiced self-quieting, it's easier to check in during these moments and know what's right. It's easier to trust your gut when you have access to it.

Research shows that our brains are constantly, subconsciously picking up on thousands of clues[17] and information. It's what we call our gut feeling. We often don't know how or why we know or feel something, but I always encourage girls to trust this intuition no matter what. As Malcolm Gladwell states in his book *Blink*[18]: *"We live in a world that assumes that the quality of a decision is directly related to the time and effort that went into making it ... We believe that we are always better off gathering as much information as possible and spending as much time as possible in deliberation. But there are moments, particularly in times of stress, when haste does not make waste, when our snap judgments and first impressions can offer a much better means of making sense of the world. Thus, decisions made very quickly can be every bit as good as decisions made cautiously and deliberately."*

The last way to understand your inner feelings is to pay attention to your urges. A story in the book The Soul's Code[19] by James Hillman best illustrates what an urge is. On amateur night at the Harlem Opera House, a skinny, awkward 16-year-old fearfully went on stage. The announcer said, "Our next person is going to dance for us …wait, hold it, hold it." There was a pause as the girl whispered to the announcer. He then said, "There has been a correction folks. She has changed her mind. She's not going to dance; she's going to sing." After that first song, the audience demanded three encores and she won first prize. With that experience under her belt, Ella Fitzgerald began her illustrious singing career.

There are times in all of our lives when we get the urge to do something. Sometimes this impulse becomes a desire, a yearning that we are drawn toward and can't get off our minds. Many times, the urges that call out for us to change direction or get out of our comfort zones are the ones that are most life-changing.

Helen Hall, a nurse practitioner, heard me give a talk in San Antonio 30 years ago and afterward, invited me to a four-day parent workshop training. I put her off for a year despite several phone call reminders. On an urge, I decided to go even though it was expensive and inconvenient. That experience created another urge in me to attend a weekend couples' retreat that my wife, Anne, resisted mightily. My passion for the retreat won out, and it changed my life. It was just the boost I needed at a time when I was leaving my general pediatrics practice to start my counseling career.

I believe we all have times like this when we are called to our fate. Discuss this concept with your kids. When they are young, it might be an urge to leave a toxic friend group, try out a new activity, go on a service trip, work with kids at a camp or spend time with the elderly. Read about my dot theory[20] and explain it to your children. Following your heart, trusting your gut and attending to your intuition means accepting experiences that cross your path because you are drawn to them. Good leaders should have the ability to access and follow their intuition. I'll leave you with this quote by Steve Chandler that describes trusting your urges:

"Listen to the clues. The next time you feel real joy, stop and think. Pay attention. Because joy is the universe's way of knocking on your mind's door. Hello in there. Is anyone home? Can I leave a message?

Good! The message is that you are happy, and that means that you are in touch with your purpose."

Chapter 8

Value Passion Where You Find It

I watched a news report about composer, virtuoso pianist and violinist Alma Deutscher. Oh, and she is 11 years old. Her dad remembers her singing practically before she started speaking. Her parents also recalled that Alma would start screaming if they tried to get her out of the car if music she loved was still playing on the radio. Alma remembers falling in love with music sometime after age 2 when she felt dumbfounded by a Strauss lullaby. "After it finished, I asked my parents, 'How can music be so beautiful?' Then I started having ideas of my own," she says. I'd just sit down at the piano. I didn't write my ideas down, I just had them in my head, and I played them. I was 4." Her dream always has been to have one of her operas debut in Vienna. In January 2017, her dream became a reality. Lucky for Alma, her parents have valued and supported her music since day one, encouraging her to follow her passion.

"The things you are passionate about are not random; they are your calling," said Fabienne Fredrickson. I wish everyone would embrace the phrase, value passion where you find it." I've heard so many stories in my counseling practice and at retreats of parents discouraging their daughters from certain careers they have an interest in, like teaching or any of the arts, (music, dance, theater, art and singing). The usual reason for the lack of support is money. One girl's parents told her they would not pay for her college if she majored in education because they told her she had more potential than that. Remember how important autonomy is for kids to

become fully engaged and persist in anything they do? You have to allow your children to follow their interests. That starts with letting them take the lead from day one when you're playing on the floor. It continues throughout their lives.

Anne Luchietto's[21] grandfather was an engineer. She used to visit his shop and was always asking questions about his tools and what he was doing. When she was 5 years old, she asked him, "Can a girl be an engineer?" He always encouraged her. When her family wanted to go to the zoo, Anne always preferred going to the museum of science and industry. Her family took her even though it was an hour's drive away. Anne was constantly taking things apart to see how they worked and then putting them back together. Because her family valued her passion, Anne went on to become a mechanical engineer at a time when women were discouraged from going into that field.

Another great story about valuing passion where you find it involves successful sculptor Olga Ayala[22]. At age 5, Olga saw her mom draw a picture of Mickey Mouse on her grocery list. She was shocked. "I thought she was like a god, and I told her she had to teach me how to do it." From that moment on, Olga always was drawing. She got in trouble at school because she had low focus and motivation for anything except art. At one parent-teacher conference, her teacher told her mom, "She's not doing her lessons. All she does is draw." Her mother's answer? "We need to buy Olga more paper at home." Olga's mom continued to inspire her and her work.

Everything kids do is prevocational in some way. Just because your 8-year-old loves to draw or dance doesn't necessarily mean she'll end up doing either as a career. But be open and willing to accept different paths your kids may be interested in, like Jennifer

Lawrence, Bobbi Brown, and Jane Goodall. Don't worry about their potential salary; instead, focus on supporting their interests so they can be engaged in their passions. That kind of experience will transfer to any future endeavors. People won't put in the 10,000 hours it requires to become masters of their field without autonomy and passion. Therefore, value passion where you find it!

Chapter 9

Social-Emotional Intelligence

Having a high level of social-emotional intelligence is critical for leadership. There is a large body of research that demonstrates the positive outcomes when social-emotional learning (SEL)[23] is taught in schools and at home. SEL includes many different skills and attitudes[24], including the ability to:
- Recognize and manage emotions
- Demonstrate care and concern for others
- Establish and maintain positive relationships
- Make responsible decisions
- Handle interpersonal situations effectively

My focus will be on the areas that directly impact the development of good leaders. In a nutshell, SEL is knowing yourself and others. More specifically, it involves good listening skills, having a win-win mentality, possessing the ability to connect and collaborate with others, pushing through fears and anxiety, overcoming adversity, and demonstrating generosity, kindness and empathy.

The next seven chapters will discuss each of these aspects of SEL and how parents can help develop these qualities in their children.

Chapter 10

Self-Awareness

"I know who I am, yesterday, tomorrow. The world may be hard, may be full of loss, but I believe in myself and what I'm doing. And that belief can carry me through the hard times; can allow me both a sense of purpose and a sense of joy."
–Victor Frankl

One key ingredient for strong leaders is that they know what makes them tick. Leaders need to have an awareness of their emotions, triggers, belief systems, and as described previously, intuition. Girls are told that they need to be authentic, but that first requires knowing who you are and what you stand for. The following are tools and strategies to help your kids develop more self-awareness.

Beliefs: I use a process called spiral of beliefs as one tool to help girls understand what they've learned to believe about themselves. Let me use an example to demonstrate this cycle.

In seventh grade, Grace suddenly was excluded from her friend group. She felt hurt, sad, confused, angry and alone. She then did what all girls do, which was go inside her head and ask herself questions like: "Why did my friends ditch me? Why don't people call me on the weekends? Why didn't anyone stand up for me?" As is always the case, she then *answered* those questions in her head as she tried to make sense of her predicament. Thoughts popped up like: "Maybe I'm not good enough, pretty enough, cool enough or important. Maybe I'm too awkward or weird. Maybe I just don't fit in." As a result of these thoughts, Grace acted differently in social situations. She became more quiet, insecure and withdrawn, which made her less noticed and connected, and her feelings intensified.

Over time, negative thoughts can become beliefs that guide our actions and behavior. Grace had a hard time trusting people, she was cautious about sharing her opinions and needs, and she stopped advocating for herself for fear of getting judged or hurt even more. She also became overly sensitive to criticism or rejection, and oftentimes missed out on people trying to include or befriend her.

From my 30 years working with girls in a retreat setting, I can guarantee that every one of your daughters has had negative experiences socially, academically or at home. Any time your daughter goes through a challenging time, gently ask questions about how she's letting it affect her. I often ask girls, "Because of what you experienced, what does that mean about you?" It's a trick question because the answer is, "Whatever you let it mean." Famous therapist Carl Jung once said, *"I am not what has happened to me; I am what I choose to become."* Remind your daughter that she is always in charge of her story. She's not in control of everything that happens to her, but she *is* in charge of what she allows it to mean about her. Adults with issues regarding closeness, trust, authority, confidence and their potential, have their seeds in the spiral of beliefs resulting from childhood adversity. The key is to consciously make better decisions about what happens to you. Eckhart Tolle's quote speaks to this process: *"The primary cause of unhappiness is never the situation but the thought about it. Be aware of the thoughts you are thinking. Separate them from the situation, which is always neutral. It is as it is."*

Meghan Markle, Duchess of Sussex[25], has a story about a challenge she faced in the seventh grade. The class had to fill out a mandatory census that required her to check a box for her race.

Self-Awareness

Since her dad was Caucasian and her mom African-American, she was confused about which box to check. Meghan felt like she'd be choosing one parent over the other and one half of herself over the other. Her teacher noticed her confusion and told her to check the box for Caucasian, explaining, "That's how you look, Meghan." She couldn't bring herself to do that, so she left it blank. She told her dad that night what had happened and his words have always stayed with her: "Meghan, if that happens again, you draw your own box." When she spoke on International Women's Day in 2015, her seventh-grade experience can be heard in her words. "Women need a seat at the table, they need an invitation to be seated there, and in some cases, where this is not available, they need to create their own table. We need a global understanding that we cannot implement change effectively without women's political participation." Fortunately, Meghan's dad helped her make good sense of her challenge.

A passage in the book *The Right Words at The Right Time Part 2*[26] illustrates the power of being in charge of your story. Nicole Hanton had an alcoholic mom who sent her at age 12 to live with her drug-addicted dad, who subsequently molested her. She returned to live with her mom and, spent her teen years taking care of her and her younger brother. Her saving grace was Lorrie, the mother of her best friend, who became the supportive adult she craved. Nicole found out that this woman had grown up with abusive parents, yet had survived and flourished. One day Lorrie gave her advice that changed her life. "You know, your life is like a train, Nicole, and you're riding down a certain set of tracks," she said "But here's the incredible thing: Even though your childhood has gone one way, you can jump that set of tracks and follow your own tracks." Nicole did just that, making different life choices than her family. Today, she works for a rape crisis center and with Child Protective Services, where she shares her mentor's invaluable advice.

Help your daughter become aware of any limiting, negative beliefs about herself that she has picked up from past experiences. This might require some personal conversations, counseling sessions, participating in personal growth retreats, or quiet, reflective journaling. Don't allow past faulty beliefs to cause your daughter to hide her light, not speak her truth or not go for it.

Self-Talk: *"It's not what you say out of your mouth that determines your life; it's what you whisper to yourself that has the most power."* Robert Kiyosaki

What we say to ourselves has a direct effect on our actions and behavior. One of my favorite quotes from Buddha explains this well: *"We are what we think; all that we are arises with our thoughts. With our thoughts we create the world. Speak or act with an impure mind and unhappiness shall follow you like the wheels that follow the ox which pulls the cart. Speak or act with a pure mind and happiness shall follow like a shadow, unshakeable."*

The female brain is wired to ruminate[27] i.e., chew on thoughts. Many girls subsequently struggle with overthinking, overanalyzing, assuming the worst, and making mountains out of molehills. First and foremost, we need to educate girls about the effects of their wiring. Read the book linked above and share it with your daughter. Her challenge is to recognize when she starts ruminating and gently redirect herself to get out of her head and refocus. I coach girls to notice body signals like a tightening in their chest or whole body, restlessness, a pounding heart, or feeling shaky. Girls also might notice an increase of negative thoughts. Teach her to gently talk to herself in those moments: "I know what I'm doing. I'm starting to ruminate. It's okay; I'm glad I caught it." Your daughter then can use tools to regain her composure, such as breath work to bring herself to the present moment and repeating a positive mantra to get rid of negativity. Girls also should stop assuming and instead, confirm that their fears are valid. For example, rather than worry that friends have moved on, ask them why you weren't invited to the sleepover.

I don't want your daughter to hold back from leadership opportunities because of limiting self-talk.

Triggers: *"The person who upsets you the most is your greatest teacher, because they bring you face-to-face with who you are."* Lynn Andrews.

A good leader needs self-control, especially when it comes to dealing with difficult people. Here's an exercise that will shine a light on why certain people are harder to deal with.

Think of a person who really gets under your skin. Note what they say or do that rankles you. With this in mind, fill in the blank: "What I see in that person that I also see in me is___." Whenever someone irritates you, she is teaching you something about yourself. She is mirroring something about you that you keep below the surface. You might see some behavior or quality in her that you also judge in yourself, but instead of using this awareness to make personal changes, you just criticize her. Sometimes, it's the opposite. You might see a quality in her that you wish you had more of and criticize her for it instead of growing in that area yourself. Another reason people may get under our skin is that they remind us of someone in our past that we have unresolved business with, i.e., lingering resentment or anger. Let me give you a personal example to make this concept clearer.

Growing up, I learned not to ask for what I needed because when I did, I was made to feel guilty with responses like, "Who do you think your father is, Nelson Rockefeller?" Or, "Do you think money grows on trees?" So, I stopped advocating for myself because I judged it as being selfish or arrogant. Thus, the people who triggered me were guys who I judged as being cocky, aggressive or boastful. Once I became aware of this unconscious belief, I worked on asking for what I wanted and developing self-advocacy. When I had grown through this issue, those types of guys no longer bothered me. It wasn't about them; they were just mirroring a place I needed some growth. This anonymous quote sums it up well: *"Your perception of me is a reflection of you; my reaction to you is an awareness of me."*

Effective leaders need thick skin because they are potential targets for criticism. Push your kids to figure out why certain peers annoy them, and help them realize these people are really just illuminating areas where they need to mature. These potential adversaries can instead be seen as their greatest teachers.

Chapter 11

Conflict Resolution and a Win-Win Mentality

South Carolina Gov. Nikki Haley gave a televised response to President Trump's State of the Union Address in January 2016 after a contentious election process. She urged her fellow Republicans to resist the siren call of the angriest, most divisive voices. "Some people think you have to be the loudest voice in the room to make a difference. That's just not true. Often, the best thing we can do is turn down the volume. When the sound is quieter, you can actually hear what someone else is saying. And that can make a world of difference."[28]

Listen to world news, and you'll quickly see that many adult leaders don't have a clue about peaceful conflict resolution. The following quote from Martin Luther King describes the lack of this skill: *"People fail to get along because they fear each other; they fear each other because they don't know each other; they don't know each other because they have not communicated with each other."* In this chapter, I will offer you ways to work through problems calmly.

- **Mirroring:** This is a form of listening where you try to see the issue from the other person's perspective. It is attempting to understand what they see and why they see it a certain way. This requires being quiet in order to really hear them. Mirroring involves one person speaking and the other just listening. The listener 'mirrors' back in their own words what they think they heard: "So what I heard you say is__. Did I get that right?" If the person responds that they heard correctly, the listener says, "Tell me more about that." The communication continues until the sender feels fully heard and understood. Sometimes it's appropriate for the sender to then become the listener so that both sides are heard. Henry Wadsworth Longfellow wrote, *"My enemy is someone whose stories I do not know."* You learn about other people's stories by mirroring.

- **Win-Win**: A win-win mentality[29] is based on mutual respect and mutual benefit. At least one person in the conflict needs to be willing to champion their adversary's interests as much as their own. Strong, mature leaders speak with courage and listen with empathy. They have the guts to advocate their position, but they care just as much about others getting their needs met as their own. One person must be willing to stay with the win-win mentality until other people trust them, at which point they are more receptive to thinking collaboratively as well. This requires a high level of inner security and strength. What becomes more important than the actual solution is the quality of the relationship.

Sibling rivalry offers opportunities to practice this skill at home. Have your kids face each other and talk through conflicts. Have child A be the listener until child B feels heard, then switch roles. Once both sides feel heard, have them find a solution where they both get their needs met, a win-win. You function as an unbiased mediator who guides them. I've taught these skills at home to my three kids, in schools, and at our retreats and camps for 30 years. Kids learn the process quickly, and you can slowly but surely back yourself out of the job of solving their fights. Practicing perspective-taking, i.e., imagining how someone else thinks or feels, promotes cognitive problem-solving and the development of empathy. Both are key ingredients for strong, sensitive leaders.

- **Cooperation:** *"A single leaf working alone provides no shade."* Chuck Page

Despite our culture's leanings toward competition, hundreds of studies over the past century have shown that collaboration and cooperative learning bring out the best in individuals and groups. Research by Johnson & Johnson[30] indicates that cooperation, compared with competitive and individualistic efforts, typically results in higher achievement and greater productivity; more caring, supportive and committed relationships and greater psychological health, social competence and self-esteem. I learned from the documentary *I Am* that Charles Darwin mentions the survival of the fittest two times and love 92 times in his books on evolution. Through his research, he believed that man's essential nature was cooperation, not competition, because it offers a better chance of survival. The authors of the book *The Athena Doctrine*[31] found that people around the world viewed leadership traits like connectedness, collaboration, compassion and a win-win mentality as necessary to make the world a better place.

We need to provide opportunities for girls to experience the difference between doing things to be the best versus making *everyone* successful. In my Strong Girls Strong World school program[32] I like to challenge girls with a game to see who in their class can make the most free throws in 30 seconds. They always do it competitively the first time, with very little teamwork or support. The result is one winner, and most of the group feels pretty blasé about the experience. I have them do it again with only one difference: I switch the intention from who can be the best to making sure everyone on their team is wildly successful. The girls brainstorm how they would do the game differently focusing on cooperation, and they then proceed to blow away their collective score from the initial trial. More importantly, the energy in the room is electric, with lots of encouragement and squeals of laughter.

Kids tend to be more cooperative in an environment where they feel respected and heard. Having a say in agreements at home or in the classroom allows kids more autonomy and control. They don't tend to push back against rules that they helped establish. As parents, engage them in discussions about chores, bedtime, homework and electronic usage. Balance your child's competitive activities with playing games where the intention is cooperation and having fun, not winning. Teach them that one of the signs of a powerful leader is making sure everyone on the team is successful. The ability to collaborate with others is essential in this increasingly interdependent world.

Chapter 12

Overcoming Fears

An old African proverb illustrates an interesting method that lions use to hunt gazelle. Young lions hide in the brush downwind from a herd of gazelle, and when they are all set, the oldest male lion in the pride goes to work. He is weak, can't run and has no teeth, but he can still growl with the best of them. The old guy sits up and roars loudly; the gazelle hear him and smell his scent, and where do you think they run? They head away from the sound and right into the teeth of the younger lions, who eat them up.

The moral of the story: In your life, when you hear the roar (feel your fear), the tendency is to run away from it and avoid the situation. This increases your anxiety even more, making it harder to proceed that time and in the future. You metaphorically get eaten up by your fears. Instead, push yourself toward and through the roar because you will find that what you are afraid of doesn't have as much 'bite' as you thought.

Remind your daughter of times when she was anxious about upcoming exams, auditions, sporting events or meeting new groups of peers. Almost always whatever she was afraid might happen didn't occur. If something did transpire, it wasn't as bad as she thought, and she handled it. That should give her the courage to 'go for the roar' in future situations.

The painter Georgia O'Keefe once said, *"I've been absolutely terrified every moment of my life, and I've never let it keep me from doing a single thing that I wanted to do."* Good leaders have the ability to overcome fears that might hold them back. That kind of courage and determination can be developed in any child.

There are many emotions that can arise when we are asked to perform in front of people or put ourselves out in front to lead: fear, excitement, worry, anticipation, joy. When Supreme Court Judge Ruth Bader Ginsburg[33] attended Cornell for undergrad, there was a male to female ratio of 4:1, resulting in many women suppressing their intelligence. She felt a lot of pressure during her Harvard Law School years as one of only nine women in her class of 500. She was afraid if she answered wrong in class, it would reflect failure for all women, but she didn't let her fears hold her back. Her perseverance resulted in her finishing in the top 5% of her class.

Teach your daughter to focus more on excitement and potential feelings of accomplishment rather than fear. Guide her to stay in the present moment versus live in the future, where our fears live. Explain that worries are about what might happen in the future, not about reality. Focusing on her breath or one sense at a time can bring her to the present moment.

Finally, watch your own emotions. Kids tend to reflect the adults around them. If your daughter looks at you and sees anxiety and trepidation, it will amplify her fear. If she looks at you and sees encouragement and an expression of "I know you can do this; I have full faith in you", she will gain confidence.

The most important reward from overcoming challenges isn't completing the final task; the real prize is simply mastering the feelings of fear leading up to it. Each time your daughter goes for the roar, pushes through her fears and overcomes an obstacle, she will gain a building block of confidence and resilience. The only way for a girl to develop these qualities is to earn it through experience.

Chapter 13

Generosity

Many years ago, when an ice cream sundae cost much less than it does today, a young boy walked into an ice cream shop and sat down at a table. As a waitress put a glass of water in front of him, he asked her the price for a sundae. "Fifty cents," she answered. The little boy pulled his hand out of his pocket and studied the coins in his hand. "How much is a dish of plain ice cream?" he asked. The increasingly impatient waitress answered, "Thirty-five cents." The lad once again counted his coins and said, "I'll just have the plain ice cream, vanilla please." The waitress brought him his ice cream, placed the bill on the table and walked away. After finishing his treat, the boy paid the cashier and left. When the waitress came back, she picked up the empty bowl and swallowed hard at what she saw. There, stacked neatly beside the empty dish, were two nickels and five pennies, her tip.

    We certainly don't want leaders who are self-centered and over-indulged. Generosity is another quality that can be developed in children. Research[34] has shown that praising character is more beneficial than praising a generous action. Acknowledging the action would sound like, "Giving your friend some of your snack was a nice thing to do." Praising character sounds like this: "I can see that you are the kind of person who loves to help others." Studies show that kids become much more generous after their character is praised versus their actions. Recognizing their positive character traits causes kids to internalize them as part of their identity and motivates them to want to earn that identity.

The Altruistic Personality Project[35] undertaken by Samuel and Pearl Oliner provided research on non-Jews who risked their lives to save Jews during the Holocaust. Rescuers internalized their social responsibility from their parents. They were disciplined by reasoning and explaining, and they were taught to consider the consequences of their misbehavior on others. Directing their attention to the distress of those hurt by their actions or inaction fueled their empathy, thus strengthening their motivation to do the right thing and avoid making that mistake in the future. These rescuers had been taught to respect all individuals, not just those like them. Parenting kids in this more authoritative style helps children become generous, moral human beings who are guided by their internal compass.

Finally, the mantra that actions speak louder than words[36] holds true with generosity. Mr. Rogers said it well, *"Attitudes are taught, not caught."* There are studies that demonstrate that philanthropic attitudes are strongly shaped by family behaviors[37]. Parents and grandparents who give and volunteer are more likely to influence their children and grandchildren to do the same. Make sure you are modeling generous behavior.

Chapter 14

Overcoming Adversity

And once the storm is over, you won't remember how you made it through, how you managed to survive. But one thing is certain. When you come out of the storm, you won't be the same person who walked in. That's what this storm's all about.
                                    –Haruki Murakami

Theologian Henri Nouwen once said, *"The great illusion of leadership is to think that man can be led out of the desert by someone who has never been there."* I highly recommend you read the book *Supernormal*[38] by Meg Jay to get the full picture on overcoming adversity. Studies have shown that those who have struggled are more likely to help others in need, are more inclusive and feel empathy for those who are suffering. Research by Mark Seery[39] revealed that people who had experienced at least some adversity were both more successful and more satisfied with their lives compared to those who experienced extremely high levels of hardship or none at all. Thus, Nietzsche's famous quote: *"In moderation, whatever does not kill us may indeed make us stronger."*

Psychiatrist Manfred Bleuler found that exposure to some hardship steels us against the impact of future adversity, what he labelled the steeling effect. It allows us to develop resilience and grit. Meg Jay found that 'supernormals,' i.e., people who have overcome adversity, are more aware of injustices in the world and often become helpers and problem-solvers at home and school. They are more willing to put on their metaphorical 'cape' and stand up for others.

Lest you are thinking that it's only the severe cases of adversity we're discussing here, research shows that up to 75% of kids and teens are exposed to at least one adverse experience in their lives. Authors of the book *Cradles of Eminence*[40] examined 400 eminent men and women, many of whom were leaders in their field. They found that three-fourths had experienced poverty, broken homes, abusive parents, alcoholism, handicaps, illness or other misfortunes. Less than 15% had been raised in supportive, untroubled homes.

Poet Dylan Thomas wrote, *"There's only one thing worse than having an unhappy childhood, and that's having a too-happy childhood."* This is why today's parents need to step back and allow their kids to experience frustrations, make mistakes, fail and overcome adversity. Kids need the opportunity to face challenges and work through obstacles without their parents doing it for them; it's the only way they will grow. They need to fight through tough times and use whatever skills they have to prevail: smarts, athleticism, family support, talent, a strong work ethic, personality, people skills, grit, etc.

I help girls at my retreats figure out the 'superpowers' they gained from overcoming adversities. They make a timeline of their life showing the challenging experiences they have faced along the way. I ask them to remember how they overcame each adversity: who was there for them, what were the words they were told or actions they took that made a difference; what did they learn from the experience; what gifts did they take away from it; what story will they tell themselves about the experience and its effect on them.

These thoughts and lessons always will be with them when facing future challenges.

Personality traits found in resilient people[41] include: good people skills, strong problem-solving skills, self-control, independence, self-confidence, humor, a sense of faith or meaning, and applicable talent to attract the attention of supporters. Perhaps the most important preventative factor found in resilience studies was that people had at least one adult who loved them and provided consistent supervision and support. As a parent, find the balance between being a loving support and solving problems for them.

Albert Einstein said it well: *"The world is a dangerous place to live; not because of the people who are evil, but because of the people who don't do anything about it."* Howard Schultz, chairman of Starbucks, used a childhood adversity to make a difference. When he was 7, his dad lost his job, which resulted in severe money constraints and household stress. The anxiety probably contributed to his death when Howard was young, leaving the family without a pension or savings. Howard overcame many obstacles before he became chairman of Starbucks. Because of what he experienced as a child, he made sure his company had an extensive health care program with benefits even for part-time workers. "I knew in my heart that if I was ever in a position where I could make a difference, I wouldn't leave people behind" he said. "Although I didn't consciously plan it that way, Starbucks has become a living legacy of my dad."[47]

Here's a great metaphor for handling adversity to share with your daughter. A girl complained to her dad that her life was miserable, and she was tired of struggling all of the time. Her father was a chef, and he took her into the kitchen. After making three pots of boiling water, he placed potatoes, eggs and ground coffee beans into the pots separately. He made his daughter watch them boil even though she became very impatient. The father took each out after 20 minutes, and asked her, "What do you see?" She answered, "Potatoes, eggs and coffee." Her dad told her to look closer as he explained.

The potatoes were soft, peeling the egg shells revealed hard-boiled eggs, and he took a sip of coffee from the last pot. "Father, what does this mean?" the girl asked. "Well, all three objects faced the same adversity, but each reacted differently," he said. "The potato went in strong, hard and unrelenting, but in boiling water, it became soft and weak. The egg was fragile, with a thin outer shell protecting its liquid interior, but after adversity, the inside of the egg became hard. However, after the ground coffee beans were exposed to boiling water, they changed the water and created something new." The father looked into his daughter's eyes and asked, "When adversity knocks on your door, how will you respond? Are you a potato, an egg or a coffee bean? Which one are you?"

How you respond to challenges is more important than the adversity faced. Joy Mangano, (42) inventor of the Miracle Mop, had all sorts of roadblocks on her path to success. Her uphill battle included poverty, discouragement, sex discrimination and divorce before she made it big. Her words are inspiring. *"Throughout my life, I was always taking care of everyone around me. And through the course of that, I lost ... I think we lose what we are. And then to find that again, and to go against all odds and have the courage to keep doing that—I wish everybody could be able to find that space within themselves."* Like Joy Mangano, solving her own problems and pushing through challenging times will allow your daughter to develop grit, resilience, determination, self-efficacy and courage. It will give her a richer perspective on what other people experience in their lives, which will allow her to see things from their point of view and be more empathetic. These qualities will make her an incredible person and leader.

Chapter 15

Connections

A university professor sent his students out into a Baltimore slum to interview 200 boys and then predict their chances for a successful future. The students were shocked at the poor conditions the boys came from, and thus predicted that 90% of the boys would someday spend time in prison. Twenty-five years later, the same professor sent another class to find out how the predictions turned out. Of the original 190 boys interviewed, only four had been imprisoned. How had these boys overcome their adverse conditions? More than 100 of them remembered one high school teacher, Miss O'Rourke, as being an inspiration in their lives. After a long search, Sheila O'Rourke was found. When asked to explain her influence over her former students, she was puzzled. "All I can say," she finally decided, "is that I loved every one of them." This story was written by John Kord Lagemann.[43]

It is imperative that our leaders have an open heart, the ability to know and to express feelings, and to be curious about others. The ability to connect with all kinds of people has benefits well beyond gaining votes. Let's dive into the value of connections for leaders and how to develop this quality in children.

Before you can relate with others, you first need a solid connection with yourself. We've covered a lot of that ground in previous chapters: knowing yourself, self-awareness, self-motivation, doing things for your own reasons, and understanding your triggers. A mature, confident, self-aware person is more able to think win-win and keep at it even if their adversary isn't there yet. They make the relationship more important than winning the disagreement.

One essential quality for an effective leader is the ability to see other people without judgment. People who feel judged won't feel safe enough to share their opinions, be themselves, think outside the box, or relate at deeper levels. This is a tough trait for kids to develop because they spend so much time in toxic environments, such as the hallways of school where judging and comparing run rampant.

Any time your child comes home with a story about a classmate, encourage them to get into that person's shoes and see the situation from their point of view. Ask why they think the other child may have acted the way they did. Teach kids that behind everyone's actions is a story that we often aren't privy to. Remind them that even if you don't know the underlying explanations behind someone's unreasonable behavior, to assume that there is a story and to treat them with understanding. Use this same line of thinking with characters in books, movies and TV shows you watch together. When you can imagine things from another's perspective, you develop more empathy and compassion for them.

A high capacity to form attachments with others is one of the foundations of resilience. Leaders who have close, supportive people in their lives are more able to sustain their efforts over time. I read a study years ago that found that having close bonds at home was one of the most important factors allowing leaders of the civil rights movement to stay committed for years. These secure bases helped leaders recover from failure and setbacks and stay determined.

I have found that many mature girls have a hard time making deep friendships until they reach their late teen years. What these girls share is an uncommon confidence and wisdom, what I would describe as being an 'old soul'.[44] They understand relationships and life at levels way beyond their years, making it hard to connect with the petty dramas that swirl around them each day at school. They refuse to play the hurtful playground politics with peers, and this sets them apart. It's a tough row to hoe because they have a tough time finding like-minded souls to connect with, leaving them feeling alone and isolated. These old souls are ahead of their time and may not find their tribe until late in high school or college when peers catch up to them.

In his book *Awareness*,[45] Anthony De Mello describes one way for these girls to approach their less mature friends. He calls it, 'I'm an ass, you're an ass.' People in their right minds don't exclude or bully friends, but most people are sleepwalking through life, even as adolescent girls. They are so caught up with fitting in and being popular, and so afraid of losing friends and being alone, that they don't act as their best selves. Therefore, don't expect more from them. No one is perfect, thus, I'm an ass, you're an ass.

Understand and accept people where they are, and you won't set yourself up to be disappointed. Mature girls who embrace this philosophy won't be so disappointed or judgmental with the insecure behavior of their peers. Encourage your daughter to find people who match their level of maturity and knowing.

These girls need safe spaces like my retreats and camps[46] or youth groups where they can be appreciated for the wisdom, courage and integrity they bring to a group. Being fully engaged in activities they are passionate about also brings them the joy and fulfillment they miss socially. Help your daughter understand why she may feel disconnected from her peers and provide affirmation for the amazing person she is.

The ability to connect depends on quality relationships with ourselves and others, and technology plays a huge role in that. Families need to create times where home is an electronics-free sanctuary for all members. The entire family can decide to form a habit of taking breaks from digital devices. Make agreements like no electronics during meals, car rides, outdoor time or when playing games. Breaks will allow everyone to become more fully present and connected.

Constant engagement with devices doesn't allow the time needed to give deeper thoughts room to bloom. College women tell me that their generation is so socially awkward, and they point to constantly being engrossed in devices as the No. 1 reason. We all become so preoccupied with what's happening 'out there' that we have no time or energy left to focus on what's going on within. Most girls I work with haven't heard from themselves in a long time. It's when we are alone and quiet that we can become more inner oriented. And that is when we can process information and experiences by asking ourselves if something is right for us. That is also when we can access our intuition so we can follow our heart. Encourage your daughter to cultivate time for reflection and to gather herself.

Your daughter can use this quiet time to check in emotionally. Girls today have become experts at being busy and distracted, and the result is that they've become disconnected from their feelings. Worries and negative thoughts pile up until they feel overwhelmed. At this point, their feelings reveal themselves as symptoms: somatic complaints about stomach aches or headaches, trouble falling asleep, snapping at people who don't deserve it, and being distracted, depressed or anxious. Encourage her to express her emotions[47] regularly by talking through them, journaling, or channeling them through art, stories, songs or poetry. Leaders who don't take care of their emotions are more likely to be reactive, angry, anxious, stressed and less present. And these are not good qualities for people who are responsible for thoughtful ideas, inspiring energy and maintaining a team. It's like oxygen masks on an airplane; parents need to put on theirs before helping their children.

Finally, a word on encouraging girls to take care of their needs. Good girl conditioning tells them to put other's needs before their own. Their automatic response to questions about what they want is often, "I don't care." Many have adopted a belief that they shouldn't have needs and that advocating for themselves is selfish. We need to teach girls how to be caring and nurturing without sacrificing their own desires. We need to reframe the good girl conditioning to a healthier model. Offer your daughters examples of people who have burned out from their jobs or an activity because they didn't take care of themselves. Brainstorm ways they can nurture themselves: taking a bubble bath, carving out alone time, drawing or painting, playing an instrument, spending time in nature, climbing trees, playing with their dog, journaling. Any time spent following their passions and interests is fulfilling and provides energy.

And by all means, model all of these ideas in your parenting, marriage and career. Children learn more by watching us than by anything that comes out of our mouths.

Chapter 16

Sacred Spaces

"When a flower doesn't bloom, you fix the environment in which it grows, not the flower."
–Alexander Den Heijer

Maggie is one of those old souls I described in the last chapter. She had never had a best friend and felt lonely a lot. She attended one of my camps and gained an important insight that changed her perspective. We often do an exercise called cross the line, where we throw out phrases like, "Cross the line if you've ever been excluded," or "Cross the line if you ever feel lonely, even when you are in a group." If the statement matches an experience you've had, you cross the line and notice how many other people relate to the same thing. Girls always are surprised by how many of their peers have experienced a similar situation. They all think they are the only ones. For Maggie, this exercise gave her permission to share and be vulnerable all week. She gained more self-awareness, confidence, coping tools and the deep connections she had been wanting.

My retreats and camps are examples of what I call 'sacred spaces'[48] which are places where girls feel safe and accepted for who they are. These communities allow them to let their hair down, get real and connect at deeper levels than they do in their everyday lives—and they are invaluable. Some girls find safety in a youth group, some when they are on family vacations where they can roam free and be a kid. Other girls can experience it in a therapy group.

Wherever it is, when girls are open to social-emotional learning, it fortifies their self-knowledge and confidence. I'm proud to say that for 29 years, my camps have been a place where girls have had the opportunity to practice leadership skills in a nonjudgmental, safe, caring environment. Be the nonjudgmental, fun, supportive home where her friends like to hang out. Provide this type of experience for your daughters whenever possible.

Chapter 17

Brave Leaders

"There will be times when standing alone feels too hard, too scary, and we'll doubt our ability to make our way through uncertainty. Someone, somewhere will say, 'Don't do it, you don't have what it takes to survive the wilderness.' This is when you reach deep into your wild heart and remind yourself, 'I AM the wilderness.'"
-Brene Brown

You hear a lot of buzz about raising girls who are brave, empowered, self-sufficient and have a voice. Many parents ask me what they can do specifically to achieve this outcome. Some girls by nature are independent, strong-minded, opinionated, free thinkers and natural born leaders. Unfortunately, these same kids often are labeled as stubborn, defiant, bossy, bitchy, uncooperative, angry and hard to deal with. When they are young, powerful kids have some rough edges that need to be smoothed out, but this needs to be accomplished without squashing their spirits.

In the following eight chapters, I will provide suggestions to help you bring out the best in strong girls. I will discuss the importance of valuing and acknowledging all of the different ways girls show leadership. The issue of teaching girls the difference between being aggressive versus assertive will be addressed, as will how to guide girls to become more assertive. I will offer you many ways to help girls learn to keep their power and to develop more self-advocacy.

Guiding your daughter to become a leader who is brave, strong, an independent thinker, assertive, influential and courageous takes some understanding, practice and guidance from the adults in her life. These next chapters will give you the blueprint for parenting girls to this end.

Chapter 18

Powerful Girls Misunderstood

Bonnie, 22, was kicked out of school in the seventh grade because of getting caught lying to teachers several times. Since then, she has developed amazing self-awareness, which allows her insight into her younger, stubborn self. "I know now it was for power, attention and control," she says. "I always felt like there were too many rules, and I was going to play by my own rules; it gave me a sense of control to do my own thing and not listen to others." Bonnie told me she used to make up silly lies all of the time because it was fun to build her own stories in her head. "I was creating my own personas," she says. "It became like an addiction."

For Kelly, her feelings of control came from bullying girls through exclusion and gossip. These actions started in the third grade, and she admits having the group follow her gave her a tremendous sense of power. "I also tried hard to hide my insecurities," she recalls. "I refused to wear the trendy, popular clothes everyone else did in order to be different, and then I made fun of girls who didn't wear my style. I wanted to set the trends and to have a voice in my world."

In *Moana*, the protagonist was drawn to the ocean and felt the urge to explore the world outside the barrier reef. The villagers saw her as different and willful. Her parents used all of their powers to constrain her, and it was only her grandmother who understood her spirit. Her destiny was to raise her village as her ancestral leaders had done before her, so it took a superhuman effort for her to break free and follow her dream.

I've met many powerful girls who are misdiagnosed as having oppositional defiant disorder or being angry. Many do indeed have some rough edges in their younger years, but I hate when adults quickly label such girls as bossy, defiant or bitchy. When they do this, they miss out on their strong spirit, creativity and leadership abilities. For instance, Kelly created her own online clothing line at age 17 because there were no classes in high school offering what she wanted to do. By her sophomore year in college, she was the fashion editor of her university's fashion magazine. Listen carefully to her words: "I have always been a 'trial and error' kind of person. I was too stubborn to listen to other people, so I always just did what I wanted. Sometimes that worked out, but a lot of times, it ended with me getting in trouble. The more I felt that my parents, teachers and friends were trying to control me, the more I pushed back to prove that I was in charge of my own life. I will always be a person that makes a lot of mistakes because that's the only way I can grow and learn. However, now I make decisions because I want to, not as a response to feeling out of power and trying to gain it back."

I have found that many powerful, independent, strong-minded girls have a sense early on of their uniqueness. They often describe a yearning to be seen, heard, respected and recognized for their strength. If they don't find suitable outlets for their power, it usually emerges as mischief, i.e., power struggles, 'mean girl' behavior, lying, risky behaviors, etc.

One thing these strong girls need are opportunities to be powerful in healthy ways. The following are ways to proactively empower kids so they don't find negative ways to feel in control.

Look for moments when they might feel vulnerable about the frustration they feel, like Bonnie and Kelly above. When they are ready to open up, be a good listener. They need to know someone understands how hard it is to channel their energy. That was Moana's grandmother's greatest gift to her. Girls need to know that despite other people's judgments, you see them for who they are: powerful and brave.[49] Have them read interesting biographies of some eminent women in the book *Smart Girls, Gifted Women*.[50]

I do not want formidable girls to hide their light because they make people around them uncomfortable. Don't allow adults, including yourself, to label your daughter as bossy or stubborn. Avoid getting into power struggles with her, especially those where you end up overpowering her to get your way. Allow her to express her creative self through unique outfits and out-of-the-box thinking and artwork. Follow her lead as much as possible in her play and activities. During grade school, try to get your daughter into classrooms with teachers who like spunky kids. She won't be a good fit with traditional, autocratic teachers.

At home, promote situations when she can be given choices and make decisions on her own. Provide opportunities for her to take risks, challenge herself and overcome obstacles on her own. Encourage her to think critically and outside the box without being judged. Offer her chances to feel valuable and can be of service. These girls are happiest when they feel like they are making a difference. I've seen powerful girls prosper when they discover causes into which they can pour their heart and soul. Strong teen girls love having jobs in the community because they can rub elbows with people of all ages and they feel more grown up and valuable.

Ask her opinion, encourage debate and respect her positions even if they are different than the rest of the family. Give her opportunities to lead, to teach you things and to set boundaries, even with you. Support her self-motivation and the ability to create, initiate, have ownership and follow her passions. Help her gain confidence by allowing her to solve her own problems and conflicts. Guide her to define power, leadership and success on her own terms. Unconditionally love and accept her for who she is, and honor and embrace her unique spirit and path. It also helps to apologize when you're wrong!

When these girls are provided places to be powerful, they relax and act as the best versions of themselves. In every situation, consider how to offer more power or control to her.

Finally, follow the example of a teacher of a 6-year-old girl who exclaimed, "My teacher thought I was smarter than I was, so I was." When your daughter looks to you, give her unconditional love for who she is. See through the external behaviors for the strong leader within.

Chapter 19

Different Kinds of Leaders

Golda Meir[51] organized a group in grade school to protest the required purchase of school books because they were too expensive for underprivileged students. She felt they were being denied the opportunity to learn. This young girl raised funds, rented space to hold a meeting, gathered a large group of girls, and then addressed the assembly. Her mom pushed her to write out the speech, but Golda refused, explaining, "It made more sense to me just to say what I wanted to say, the speech from my heart." Years later, she went on to lead Israel during the Yom Kippur War and became its fourth prime minister, the first and only woman to have held the office. I wonder if her teachers valued her courage or judged her as being a troublemaker.

"The simple act of caring is heroic." Edward Albert

Tamille, 16, felt terrible as she watched a group of friends tease a classmate with Down syndrome. She had the guts to tell them to stop, but they all just walked away laughing. Tamille decided to do something about this injustice. She and some like-minded friends organized a separate prom for disabled students in the area. They all got dressed in formalwear and danced the night away. She told me she had never felt so happy and valuable.

Our culture values a very narrow type of hero, and this needs to change. Young Golda Meir is known for her courage in leading Israel, but I believe her grade school protest was even more heroic.

People who most often are recognized for bravery are soldiers, first responders and athletes. Movies, TV shows, and books point to people who stand up to and battle physically larger opponents. The problem is that very few girls will ever experience these trials in real life. And what about the women and men who wield pens, books, whistles, scalpels or an ear to listen? What about kids like Tamille who go under the radar at school when they have the guts to make a difference even when it's not popular? Why do we not recognize teachers, coaches, doctors, social workers and counselors? Because of this exclusion, what are we teaching children about what's really important and what we should value most?

When I ask girls who at school holds the most power and are seen as leaders, they list: student council officers, team captains, top athletes, Queen Bees, the prettiest and most popular girls, and 'good girls.' But there are numerous other ways girls can exhibit leadership qualities. Listed are a few examples:

- Don't give their power away to others (see Chapter 3)
- Stand up for themselves and others
- Don't care what others think about them regarding clothes, friends, interests, etc.
- Advocate for themselves and are persuasive
- Are an influencer in positive ways
- Don't allow words or gossip to bother them
- Set clear, firm boundaries
- Are inclusive and kind to everyone
- Don't allow themselves to get sucked into drama or gossip
- Handle conflicts directly and peacefully
- Listen to and meet other's concerns and needs
- Hold their peers accountable

Different Kinds of Leaders

- Willing to take risks, go out of their comfort zone and make mistakes
- Push past fears and go for the roar
- Willing to take charge and make things happen
- Trust their intuition with decisions
- Good problem-solver
- Let others lead; supportive follower
- Make space for others
- Energetic and happy; lift others up
- Safe for all to confide in them
- Find unique, deeper meaning in things
- Focused on making everyone successful
- Committed to bringing their community together

Acknowledge and affirm these qualities in your daughter. Point out examples of different types of courage and leadership you see in books, movies and the news. Recognize kids like Tamille and adults who serve our world as nonviolent peacekeepers, good listeners, community builders, healers, teachers, counselors and mentors. Look for people who lead with compassion, collaboration, inclusion, humility, connectedness and a win-win vision. Kids get overwhelmed with pseudo-important people on reality shows and in the media. Make sure they read the stories of truly courageous people like Golda Meir.

So many girls exhibit the qualities listed above, yet are not considered leaders. It will be easier for them to embrace their power if it is reflected back to them. What you notice and affirm in your daughter and others, you tend to get more of in return, including these different types of leadership.

Chapter 20

Paradigm Shift About Courage

Booker T. Washington, educator and founder of Tuskegee University, was walking down the street one day when he passed the mansion of a wealthy elderly woman, to whom he was nothing more than a black person. He heard her call out, "Come here boy. I need some wood chopped." Without a word, Washington pulled off his jacket, picked up the ax and went to work, not only cutting a pile of wood but carrying it into the house. A moment after he left, a servant told the women, "Ma'am, that was professor Washington, president of the university." Mortified, the woman went to the school to apologize. Washington replied, "There's no need for apologies, madam. I'm delighted to do favors for my friends." The woman became one of Tuskegee's most generous supporters[52].

Washington refused to be disturbed by insult or persecution, and thus kept his peace of mind. He didn't take the disrespect personally, which allowed him to keep his power. He lived out one of his most repeated mantras: "I shall allow no man to belittle my soul by making me hate him." I want every girl to deal with relationship aggression in this way.

"How beautiful it is to stay silent when someone expects you to be enraged." Kushand Wizdom

The following is an insightful story about Buddha demonstrating a balance of feminine and masculine leadership energy. One day as he was teaching his followers, an angry general came storming up, screaming at Buddha. The holy man sat still, showing no reaction to the soldier. At one point, the soldier drew his sword and threatened Buddha, but he remained calm and detached. Eventually, the general left. Buddha's followers asked him why he didn't get upset and respond to the man, and his answer contained great wisdom. "If a man offers you a gift, and you refuse to accept it, to whom does the gift belong?" His followers answered, the person who offered the gift. Buddha said, "It is the same with anger, criticism and disrespect. If I do not accept what he is saying, then the words belong to him, not me."[53] That, my friends, is true freedom. I wish every girl could exhibit that kind of power.

"Women must read, hear and see the stories of other women who have reinvented themselves in desperate situations to appreciate the profundity of our own lives, to know that we are not alone, and to realize that facing our truth and our pain is a heroic act of strength, not weakness." Kathleen Noble

We need a paradigm shift regarding what leadership looks like. It is imperative that we provide our daughters with examples of more inclusive, compassionate leaders. Point them out any chance you get so they have proper role models.

Chapter 21

Step into a Leader's Shoes

When I asked 9-year-old Lauren what she wanted to do when she grew up, she said, "I might want to be a veterinarian because I love animals. I used to think I wanted to be president of the United States, but I don't want everybody yelling at me all of the time."

Becoming president used to be one of parents' highest aspirations for their children, but I'm not so sure that remains true today. The hostility and disrespect among politicians and voters is a turn-off to most young people like Lauren who might have an interest in serving their country. Kids frequently hear adults criticizing and judging leaders of all kinds, which can discourage them from taking on leadership roles. They don't see the point in putting themselves in situations where everyone would condemn and judge them. In the current environment, how can we best educate our kids about having the courage to step to the front and lead?

The most impactful thing parents can do is encourage their kids to put themselves in a leader's shoes rather than jump to criticize them. Allow open conversations in your home where everyone can share how *they* would handle various situations as a principal, teacher, coach, president or team captain. Have kids imagine themselves in that role and see themselves as a leader instead of a victim. Teach kids to be critical thinkers and problem solvers instead of passive complainers and blamers.

We need to educate young adults how to debate with authority and respect. You can watch documentaries about world issues with them and then have open discussions. A father told me recently that once a week at dinner, he has each of his children give a spontaneous 5-minute talk to persuade the rest of the family on a topic the dad chooses. What a great way to practice advocating for a cause. As a kid, I used to love listening to my parents and their friends discuss politics at our holiday meals. I learned it's OK to have strong opinions, how to put them out there, and how to not take disagreement personally. Research has shown that having kids reflect on victims who have suffered an injustice makes it more likely they will speak up to right wrongs done to others. I believe the same is true about leadership.

Chapter 22

Assertive vs. Aggressive

Dani asked Aisha if they could handle an issue during one of our circle times. She was worried Aisha might be mad because she had reminded her after lunch that it was their day to clean off the tables. Dani noticed Aisha talking with friends instead of pitching in. Her fear that she had overstepped her bounds is a common fear of girls as they grapple with leadership roles. We acknowledged Dani for holding her teammate accountable, a sign of a strong leader.

It is critical that we teach girls the difference between being assertive versus being aggressive. Good girl conditioning causes most girls to err on the side of not speaking up and setting boundaries because they're afraid of making friends mad, losing friends or being seen as a bitch. Assertive leaders need to be able to ask for what they want, refuse what they don't, hold others accountable, speak their truth with authority, set boundaries and say no. The following are ways to teach your daughter about assertiveness.

Awareness: Help girls become aware of the good girl conditioning that can limit their behavior. Discuss where these beliefs came from and how they affect their choices and actions.

Role playing: This is a tool I use at my retreats and camps to let girls practice self-assurance. I give them a situation that requires action, and they have to show the group how they could handle it passively, aggressively and assertively. Examples include when a friend tells you they don't want you hanging out with anyone else; a sibling talks loudly on the phone when you're watching a movie;

you overhear two people talk badly about your friend behind her back.

You can try a similar tactic at home. Have your daughter show you how she handled an incident with a friend, and then give her feedback. Look for the following: Did she stay calm but firm? Did she use 'I' statements about how she feels and what she wants? Did she use an assertive voice and body language (stand tall, make eye contact and maintain a serious expression)? Did she convey confidence and determination? Did she refuse to threaten, pressure or put the other person down? Did she respect the other person's feelings and needs? Have her practice until she comes across in a powerful and respectful manner.

Cost: Help your girls become aware of what happens when they don't set boundaries. The result is feeling angry, frustrated, resentful, hopeless, powerless, overpowered and like a victim. Girls also don't feel heard, understood or get what they want. They may react to these feelings by avoiding people, shutting down, overreacting with anger, passively creating drama or gossiping about their adversary, or deciding that their needs are not important and thus they are not important. Getting in touch with these emotions can create the motivation to handle it differently.

Experiments: I love to have girls try small experiments to change their behavior. They might try asking for what they want with waitresses, cashiers or other people they don't know and probably will never see again. Ask them to order off the menu themselves and then check out what happens. It makes them more satisfied with their meal, so they're more motivated to give a good tip, which makes the waiter feel good. Everybody is happy, which goes against their belief that getting what you want will upset others.

Assertive vs. Aggressive

I encourage young girls to start small and accumulate evidence that shows them the power in being assertive.

Indirect lessons: Once again, use examples you find in books, TV shows, movies, or with friends to teach skills and illustrate your points. Ask your daughter what she notices when someone does and does not set boundaries or act assertively. Have her get inside the character's shoes to see and feel what they might be experiencing. Ask her how the person could have handled it more assertively and effectively. I love indirect lessons because the spotlight is not on them, so they often are more open about discussing the situation.

Chapter 23

Keeping Your Power

The most common way people give up their power is by thinking they don't have any.
—Alice Walker

Gabby's best friends ditched her in seventh grade. She decided it must be because she was weird and not good enough, and she thought she'd never fit in. These beliefs caused her to not set boundaries, be abused by friends and guys, and to drift through the hallways of school trying to avoid being noticed. She gave her power away to those girls.

We've touched on it some already, but below are even more examples of how girls can keep their power. It may seem obvious, but successful leaders are ones who know how to maintain control.

Know what you want and ask for it. Whenever someone asks what you want, stop yourself from giving the automatic response of, "I don't care. Whatever you want." Experiment with pausing before you answer to figure out how to speak your truth. From what girls have told me, when they do this, usually no one gets upset and they get what they ask for. So everybody is happy. Every girl should believe her needs are important.

State your opinion and needs with authority. You'll need to teach your daughter that when she puts her ideas out there, she will be judged. Some people will admire her spunk, and others will judge her as being too forceful or opinionated. It's important that she knows this in advance so she is ready for various reactions to her advocacy. But she can learn to not care what others think or let their judgments affect her. If she understands that everyone sees and handles situations based on their own past experiences, it will help her not take things personally. That will be critical if she's in a position where she is taking charge and going against the grain.

Take responsibility.: *I was told I was dangerous. I asked why, and their response was, "Because you don't need anyone." I smiled. Unknown*

Girls need to be told to not use victim words like, "She made me feel___" or "I need ___ to make me happy." Teach your daughter to take full responsibility for her feelings, reactions and actions even if it seems clear the other person was at fault. This will allow her a tremendous sense of freedom in knowing that no one can *make* her feel anything and that she is always in charge of how she reacts to people and situations.

Handle conflicts directly. I discussed the mechanics of how to do this in chapter 12. There is great power in communicating directly with people instead of making assumptions, creating drama or avoiding the situation. Girls who are straightforward with peers feel the confidence that comes with standing up for yourself and taking care of yourself.

Don't compare yourself. This starts to become a problem for most girls by sixth or seventh grade. I teach them that it's a trap because, at least in their minds, they will always find someone prettier, thinner, smarter or better in some way. This leaves girls feeling discouraged and less than. I encourage girls to do it differently. If they see something they admire in someone, they should acknowledge that person for it. They shouldn't make it about them, especially with negative comparisons; instead, they should keep the energy where it belongs, with the person they appreciate.

Boundaries. Anger often arises when boundaries are crossed, you've been wronged or there is an injustice. Teach your daughter to make the connection that her anger is a sign that it's time to set a boundary. She should use the emotion to inspire action, resist the current state of affairs or overcome an obstacle. I love this quote by William Arthur Ward: *"It is wise to direct your anger toward problems, not people; to focus your energies on answers, not excuses."* I also work with girls to help them learn to say no without an explanation. As noted in the assertiveness chapter, girls often need practice through role playing, which would be helpful in learning how to set boundaries so they know how to come across firm and clear.

Rethink negative beliefs.: Gabby's story demonstrated how negative experiences can cause girls to make faulty decisions about themselves. Restoring her power meant she had to reconsider her beliefs about why her friends left her. In reality, they were insecure and inappropriately used their power. Becoming in charge of her story and what the experience meant about her was extremely empowering for Gabby, and it will be for your daughters as well.

Intuition: Rita Mae Brown once said, *"I think the reward for conformity is that everyone likes you except yourself."* That really resonates with adolescent girls. Another way girls can keep their power is to shut out all of the external noise and pressures of what others are saying and doing and instead, make decisions by trusting their intuition. It takes a tremendous amount of maturity and self-confidence to think for yourself and not follow the crowd. Help your daughter become conscious of her inner voice and trust her gut.

Find your passions. Doing things you love brings joy and fulfillment. Allow your daughter to pick activities she feels called to do; that's when she will become fully engaged and derive the most pleasure. Besides making her happy, she also will find supportive, like-minded people.

Find your tribe. Good leaders always have a strong support system. Impress upon your daughter the importance of surrounding herself with loving, supportive people. I often have our campers make a list of all of the qualities they want in a best friend. They typically mention traits like: kind to everyone, inclusive, doesn't gossip or get into drama, has my back, doesn't talk behind my back, fun, shares common interests, etc. I then have them do three things with the list. First, I ask them to make sure they are living those qualities because we tend to attract people who match our level of psychological health. Second, I have them compare the list with who they hang out with the most. For many girls, this is a real eye-opener, as many of their best friends don't match the list. Third, and most important, I tell them to be aware of who at their school actually does match their list. They should base their judgments on behaviors, not superficial qualities or past reputations. Then it's up to them to befriend the people who match their list. I tell the girls that while they need to be kind to everyone, it's more than OK to be picky about who they hold close. They deserve supportive friends who give as much to the relationship as they do and who emit positive energy. This is how to find a supportive tribe.

Redefine power: As mentioned in chapter one, help your daughter define power and leadership on her own terms. Teach her about the archetypal feminine and masculine energies and how to create a healthy balance. Guide her over time to also let go of our culture's unrealistic standards of success and to define what triumph means for her. Creating her own benchmarks and expectations will cause less pressure and keep her focus inward.

Be a good model. Sandra Day O'Connor was unanimously voted in to become the first woman on the U.S. Supreme Court in 1981. She grew up on a cattle ranch, learning to shoot guns and drive a truck before she reached the age of 10. She became tough, self-reliant and a good listener with a great understanding of people. Her dad was a cowboy who was described as tough, rough and harsh. Her mom was elegant and tough in a different way. She learned to deal with her husband by not taking his bait or allowing herself to be bullied. Sandra apparently learned a lot by watching her mom. She ascended into a career that at the time was a man's world, but she had the ability to not take things personally and to give as much as she received[54]. Like with Justice O'Connor, kids learn more by what we do than by what we say, so be sure you model keeping *your* power.

Chapter 24

Un-Words

All of man's miseries derive from not being able to sit quietly in a room alone.
—Blaise Pascal

Unreachable, undisturbed, uninterrupted, unleashed, unaffected, unlimited, unwavering and unconditional are not just words; they are a way of being that will allow your daughters to transcend any limiting stereotypes, peer pressure and cultural standards. Encourage these virtues through your words, actions and how you parent. These are essential tools for influential trailblazers.

Unreachable: Spending time alone, unreachable, and undisturbed allows stressed-out girls a chance to breathe, refuel and focus on the crucial work of transformation they are undergoing in adolescence, whether they are aware of it or not. It is only in these quiet moments that girls can gather themselves, soul-search, and have access to their feelings, needs and intuition.

Unlimited: *If you hear a voice within you say, 'You cannot paint,' then by all means paint, and the voice will be silenced."* Vincent Van Gogh

Educate your daughter about limiting stereotypes society tries to impose on them, unrealistic standards of perfection, and narrow definitions about motherhood and careers. Guide them to define what 'having it all' means for them, and then encourage them to follow their heart.

Unaffected: The happiest girls I know are the ones who don't care what other people think about them. They don't give their power away by allowing disrespectful words or gossip to hurt their feelings, and they make decisions based upon their internal compass regardless of what their peers and society tells them.

Unwavering: One of the most important qualities girls can leave home with is grit,[55] the ability to persevere despite hardship and challenges. Allow them to get frustrated, problem-solve, dig deep and overcome obstacles in order to develop the conviction that they can achieve their goals and dreams. Eleanor Roosevelt said it well: *"Develop skin as tough as a rhino's hide. You cannot take anything personally. You cannot bear grudges. You must finish the day's work when the day's work is done. Don't be easily discouraged. Take defeat over and over, pick yourself up and go on."* Strong leaders need resilience.

Unleashed: Oliver Wendell Holmes was quoted as saying, *"The mind, once expanded to the dimensions of bigger ideas, never returns to its original size."* Unleashed is a willingness to get out of your comfort zone, take risks, make waves, go against the grain, speak out against injustice, and be fully you no matter the crowd or circumstances. Acknowledge your daughter whenever she challenges herself, no matter the result. Celebrate mistakes as opportunities to learn and grow. Encourage her to go for the roar. Remind her that the juiciest fruits are out on the skinniest limbs.

Unconditional: Having people in their corner who unconditionally love and support them allows girls to believe in themselves during times of self-doubt and insecurity. Girls need to know that their parents believe in them, especially when they are struggling or making mistakes. Parents and mentors can hold a higher vision of girls when they can't yet see it in themselves.

Chapter 25

Opportunities for Advocacy

Second-grader Siri came home from school upset because the teacher yelled a lot that day. She had never been the target of the scolding, but she told me that it hurt her heart to see other kids suffer. I saw Siri in my counseling practice because she was refusing to go to school. I encouraged her to sit down with her teacher and share how she felt and what she wanted. Her mom went with her but sat silently in the back to allow Siri to speak for herself. Her teacher listened and told her she was glad that she shared her feelings. She promised to work on not yelling at her students and at a follow-up visit two weeks later, she had kept her word. Siri felt incredibly empowered by this experience.

You won't have to look far to find opportunities for girls to speak their truth. There are plenty of everyday challenges to allow practice. The following are examples of how kids can practice advocacy.

- **Siblings**: It's easy to fall into the habit of solving your children's fights. Instead, use the ideas I put forward in chapter 11 to guide siblings to voice their needs and work out win-win agreements with each other. You will need to speak up for young children until they are around 4 or 5 years of age. After that point, push them to speak on their own behalf, even if their sibling is several years older. Refrain from overprotecting the younger sibling and empower them instead. If they learn to stand toe-to-toe in this manner with their older

sibling, you'll have prepared them to handle anyone in the neighborhood or at school.
- **Parents:** Redirect whining by telling your child to tell you what they want. If they can't calm down and use their normal voice, tell them to find you when they've calmed down. In my book, *Keeping Your Family Grounded When You are Flying by the Seat of Your Pants*,[56] I wrote an entire chapter on how to run family meetings. These are an excellent place for kids to learn to voice their concerns, needs and ideas in a collaborative process. Everyone stands on equal ground, and you provide a safe place for all to feel safe to speak their truth and debate issues.
- **Out in public:** There are so many chances for kids to speak for themselves when you're out and about. This can be ordering at restaurants or the ice cream shop, buying tickets at movie theaters, handling their ticket at the airport, or asking for directions when traveling. If they become afraid, remind them of the lion story in chapter 12 and to go for the roar. Sometimes it might be that they don't get ice cream at the store because they weren't willing to tell the person what they wanted. If you start when they're young, it sets the precedent that you are unwilling to do for them what you know they can do for themselves.
- **Teachers:** In my experience, even when things don't change after conversations like Siri's, kids still feel more confident for having had the courage to go through the process. It is such a confidence builder for a kid to sit face-to-face with an adult and advocate for change.
- **Coaches:** When my son TJ was a senior in high school, he became unhappy with his ice time during hockey games.

Opportunities for Advocacy

I was so tempted to call the coach on his behalf, but fortunately allowed him to do it on his own. Looking back now as a 34-year-old, he remembers how empowering it was for him to advocate for himself even though his ice time didn't increase much. At the senior banquet at the end of the year, his coach said he had never had a player talk to him so directly and respectfully. To this day, TJ uses the courage from experiences like that to deal with professors and bosses. Allowing your daughters to advocate for themselves like this can become the gift that keeps on giving.

- **Professors:** If you haven't let go of micromanaging your kids by their high school graduation, then at least definitely start when they go off to college. I remember at a college orientation for my daughter, the dean advised parents to stay out of the room where their child would be signing up for their first-semester classes. Unbelievably, when we arrived, my wife and I saw many parents demanding to be allowed in the room, even yelling at the administrators. Many of their kids came out of the room crying because they had no clue how to manage themselves. College professors tell me they get phone calls every day from disgruntled parents complaining about their children's grades. If there are any problems with 'undeserved' bad grades, parking tickets or roommate squabbles, please empower your children to solve these challenges themselves. Better yet, start turning over self-advocacy little by little throughout childhood so that the challenges they face at age 18 are less daunting.
- **Other adults:** I've encouraged many kids over the years to set boundaries with relatives. Some kids shy away from grandparents who demand hugs and kisses immediately upon entering their home. I encourage kids to let them know

how they feel and to speak up. When kids at my camps have a problem with one of our staff, we urge them to have a 'courageous conversation' or a 'con-res'(conflict resolution) to handle the issue (see chapter 11). Empowering your daughter to handle these sorts of issues herself allows advocacy to become second nature and less fear laden.

- **Friends:** Last but not least, teach girls the skills to handle conflicts peacefully and effectively at home so it will carry over into friendship struggles. The female brain[57] is wired to communicate and connect. For 150,000 years, women who were connected in a group had a much better chance of surviving. If prehistoric women got into a conflict and were kicked out of the tribe, they died. That is exactly how girls describe it when they lose friends; it feels like a death. So, they avoid it like the plague. Girls will put up with abuse and apologize when they've done nothing wrong, anything to preserve the friendship.

That's why it's imperative that we teach them the conflict resolution skills described in chapter 11. When a conflict arises, it's easier for most girls to push their feelings aside and act like it's no big deal than it is to handle it directly. But those feelings tend to fester and then leak out in relationship aggression and drama. Girls need to push through their fears about making the other person mad or losing the friendship and just do it. A true friend will listen and want to work it out. People who get angry and cause more drama are showing you what kind of friend they are, a lower- level, untrustworthy one. I tell girls to never let anyone get comfortable with disrespecting them. If your daughter has had lots of practice working through issues with you and siblings at home, she's more likely to take those skills into other relationships.

Chapter 26

Where Do We Go from Here

"Each time a man stands up for an ideal, or acts to improve the lot of others, or strikes out against injustice, he sends forth a tiny ripple of hope. And crossing each other from a million different centers of energy and daring, those ripples build a current, which can sweep down the mightiest walls of oppression." Robert Kennedy

Grace, 17, came to see me because she was experiencing high levels of anxiety. Making decisions stressed her out the most. She was extremely sensitive to not making people mad or disappointing them. We discovered that the root of her problem was from an experience in middle school. Grace used to be a free spirit who wore offbeat clothes and purple sneakers. But that ended when her friend group ditched her in sixth grade. She became withdrawn and lost her self-confidence. Grace became so afraid she would say or do something stupid and be excluded again that she stopped speaking up. Although it kept her safe, she now was tired of being invisible. After attending a week of my summer camp, she regained her confidence. I saw Grace a month later, and she was all smiles as she exclaimed, "Check it out. I'm back to my purple shoes!" Sure enough, she was wearing a pair of purple sneakers that screamed, "I don't care what other people think about me anymore!"

Whether or not your daughter becomes the leader of the free world is less important than her acquiring the skills to carve out the life she deserves and desires. Girls need to learn to make decisions based on their own moral compass and to set their own bar. They need to know how to quiet their minds, go inward, connect with and trust their intuition and urges, and use that to guide their choices.

Leading a group or leading a good life requires the ability to connect and collaborate with others, push through fears and anxiety, overcome adversity, and demonstrate generosity, kindness and empathy. Helping girls develop strong self-awareness will allow them to establish and maintain healthy relationships and to handle interpersonal situations effectively. Leaders need to have a handle on their emotions and what triggers them, and to find healthy ways to express their feelings. Bottom line, to lead a family, business, government or any group of people, you need to know what makes you tick, and to understand why other people behave the way they do as well. We can guide kids to develop high social-emotional intelligence.

We learned about powerful women like Maj. Gen. Orna Barbivai, Ruth Bader Ginsberg, Golda Meir, Jane Goodall and Sandra Day O'Connor who transcended limiting stereotypes and became prominent leaders. Just as important, we learned the value of acknowledging girls for the many ways they exhibit courage and leadership day by day at home and at school. You can help girls become aware of any potential constraints that might impede their growth. Parents can appreciate and guide powerful young girls who have rough edges without dampening their spirit. We can use everyday examples, both direct and indirect, to demonstrate ways girls and women keep their power and give it away. Girls need practice advocating for themselves, setting boundaries and being assertive in all of their relationships. We can help them learn from examples of women *and* men who exhibit a balanced blend of feminine and masculine leadership qualities.

John Lennon told of a time as a five-year-old when he acted assertively. His mother always told him that happiness was the key to life. When he went to school, they asked him what he wanted to be when he grew up. He wrote down 'happy.' They told John he didn't understand the assignment, and he told them they didn't understand life. Every girl has that strength and confidence within them.

The result of all of this? Girls who want more can become more and create more than what is expected from limiting cultural stereotypes.

One of my favorite quotes by Stephen Covey describes this phenomenon. *"When you engage in work that taps your talent and fuels your passion; that rises out of a great need in the world that you feel drawn by conscience to meet; therein lies your voice, your calling, your soul's code, your destiny."*

We can guide girls to grow into their destinies. To live out that quote, girls must be inner directed, have a high sense of personal awareness, have access to their intuition and urges, and possess the courage to get out of their comfort zones and go for it. We can teach girls that sometimes people around them won't understand or validate their journey, but that's OK because it's not their journey. That is how you raise a leader.

Finally, words for us all to live by. *"One word can end a fight, one hug can start a friendship, one smile can bring unity, one person can change your entire life."* Israelmore Ayivor

And if I may add to this quote: One girl can change the world.

Notes: Leadership book

1) *The Athena Doctrine:* John Gerzema and Michael D'Antonio
2) Plan-International.org: Taking the lead
3) *The Curse of the Good Girl;* Rachel Simmons
4) *Mindset: The New Psychology of Success;* Carol Dweck
5) *The Female Brain*; Luanne Brizendine
6) *Where You Go is Not Who You'll Be*; Frank Bruni
7) *Punished by Rewards: The Trouble with Gold Stars, Incentive Plans, A's, Praise, and Other Bribes;* Alfie Kohn
8) *Drive;* Daniel Pink
9) *The Talent Code*; Dan Coyle
10) *Jane;* Documentary on Jane Goodall
11) *The Female Brain*; Luanne Brizendine
12) "The Power of Taylor Swift"; *Time Magazine*, November 24, 2014
13) *Callings: The Purpose and Passion of Work*; (Dorothy Wharburton Story) Dave Isay
14) *How Does Nature impact Our Wellbeing?* Takingcharge.csh.umn.edu
15) *Last Child in the Woods*; Richard Louv
16) *Why Kids Need to Spend Time in Nature*; Danielle Cohen; childmind.org
17) *The Gift of fear and Other Survival Signals that Protect Us from Violence*; Gavin de Becker
18) *Blink: The Power of Thinking Without Thinking*; Malcolm Gladwell
19) *The Soul's Code*; James Hillman

20) *Letters from My Grandfather: Timeless Wisdom For a Life Worth Living*; Tim Jordan M.D.
21) *Callings: The Purpose and Passion of Work*; (Anne Luchietto story) Dave Isay
22) *Callings: The Purpose and Passion of Work*; (Anne Luchietto story) Dave Isay
23) Social Emotional Learning Impact; casel.org
24) Social and Emotional Learning Programs That Work; bestevidence.org
25) Megan Markle story; *Elle Magazine* July 2015
26) *The Right Words at the Right Time Part 2;* Marlo Thomas
27) *The Female Brain;* Luanne Brizendine
28) *Where You Go is Not Who You'll Be*; (Nikki Hayley story) Frank Bruni
29) *The 8th Habit: From Effectiveness to Greatness*; Stephen Covey
30) *Cooperation and Competition: Theory and Research;* David Johnson and Roger Johnson
31) *The Athena Doctrine*: John Gerzema and Michael D'Antonio
32) Strong Girls, Strong World School Program; www.drtimjordan.com
33) RBG Documentary; Magnolia Pictures 2018
34) *Raising a Moral Child*; Adam Grant, nytimes.com, April 11, 2014
35) *Ordinary Heroes*; Samuel Oliner; yesmagazine.org Nov. 5, 2001

36) *Generosity in Children: Immediate and Long-Term Effects of Modeling, Preaching, and Moral Judgment;* J. Philippe Rushton; J. of Personality and Social Psychology 1975, Vol. 3
37) *Parents, Grandparents Influence Charitable Giving and Volunteering of Children;* Vanguard Charitable; business.com
38) *Supernormal: The Untold Story of Adversity and Resilience;* Meg Jay
39) *Whatever Does Not Kill Us: Cumulative Lifetime Adversity, Vulnerability, and Resilience*; Mark Seery; J Pers Soc Psychol. 2010 Dec.
40) *Cradles of Eminence: Childhoods of More Than 700 Famous Men and Women*; Victor Goertzel
41) *Supernormal: The Untold Story of Adversity and Resilience;* Meg Jay
42) Joy Mangano: biography; biography.com and from the movie Joy
43) *Everyday Greatness: Inspiration for a Meaningful Life*; Stephen Covey
44) *Why Amazing Girls Feel Lonely*; Tim Jordan M.D. https://drtimjordan.com/2016/06/amazing-girls-feel-lonely/
45) *Awareness*; Anthony De Mello
46) www.campweloki.com
47) *Sleeping Beauties, Awakened Women: Guiding the Transformation of Adolescent Girls;* Tim Jordan M.D.
48) Sacred Spaces: podcast by Tim Jordan M.D. Raising Daughters; https://drtimjordan.com/2018/05/054-sacred-spaces/

49) *Girls Who March to a Different Drum Change the World*; Tim Jordan M.D. blog at https://drtimjordan.com/2016/12/girls-march-different-drum-change-world/
50) *Smart Girls, Gifted Women*; Barbara Kerr
51) *The Soul's Code: In Search of Character and Calling;* James Hillman
52) Booker T. Washington chops wood: https://sermons.faithlife.com/sermons/103403-booker-t.-chops-wood
53) *Song of the Bird*; Anthony De Mello
54) CBS This Morning; (Sandra Day O'Connor story) Interview March 19, 2019
55) *Grit: The Power of Passion and Perseverance*; Angela Duckworth
56) *Keeping Your Family Grounded When You Are Flying by the Seat of Your Pants;* Tim Jordan M.D.
57) *The Female Brain*; Luanne Brizendine

About the Author

Tim Jordan M.D. is a developmental and behavioral pediatrician who has worked with girls and young women for over 30 years through his counseling practice, personal growth and leadership development weekend retreats and summer camps (Camp Weloki), and his Strong Girls Strong World School Program. He has given talks to parents and girls in 18 countries and throughout the US. He has published five books, articles, blogs and podcasts as well as being a media consultant for 25 years. Tim has been married for 38 years and is the father of three adult children along with one grandson.

For more information on Dr. Jordan and his blogs, podcasts, camps, and other educational materials, go to his website at www.drtimjordan.com

Made in the USA
Columbia, SC
24 June 2025

59820527R00071